Bonaparte & Brimstone

A life of mixed fortunes in the Royal
Navy and merchant service

Simon Francis Brown

Bonaparte & Brimstone

Published by The Conrad Press Ltd. in the United Kingdom 2023

Tel: +44(0)1227 472 874

www.theconradpress.com

info@theconradpress.com

ISBN 978-1-915494-35-1

Typesetting and Cover Design by: Charlotte Mouncey, www.bookstyle.co.uk

The Conrad Press logo was designed by Maria Priestley.

Printed and bound in Great Britain by Clays Ltd, Elcograf S.p.A.

Contents

Introduction

Growing up, John Monk lived in our dining room. An old watercolour of his merchant brig, the *Monk*, hung above the grey stone fireplace, and his flintlock pistols and daggers were arranged beneath it on the mantelpiece. As children, when no one was looking, my brother and I liked to fire the unloaded pistols at each other. They still had the flints in them and gave a satisfying spark. My favourite was the smaller of the two, with a retractable bayonet that would pop out like a 1950s flick knife if I pulled on the trigger guard. My mother polished the dagger sheath regularly, in a way I doubt anyone does any more, slowly rubbing through the gold-plating in her determination to keep everything shining.

Beyond these artefacts, I knew very little about their original owner, except that he was an ancestor of some sort. My father had inherited John's papers from an uncle, but I don't believe he ever looked at them and they stayed tucked away in a black metal box, along with other family documents. My father passed away several years ago after a series of debilitating strokes, and the faded picture of the brig now hangs in my own study.

As I began carefully sorting through the bundles of papers, my first response was delight at how old they were. Many were letters, hand-written in loopy scrawls, with wax stamps to seal them. Most took some effort to read. Some were official documents, confirming John's diligent and sober employment on different Royal Navy ships of the line. There were commendations from captains and admirals that John had gathered as he sought promotion from the Admiralty, personal notes from lords and ladies, and intimate family letters, describing pets, children, and neighbours. There was even a diary from 1824, a passenger's record of a stormy journey to Italy on a merchant brig of which John was master.

As I worked through them, the centuries between me and the fragile papers began to fall away, and a more rounded picture of a man and his life started to emerge. There were stories of the war with Napoleon Bonaparte, storms, shipwreck and mutiny, even tales of piracy and a fatal duel; but behind this, I found a life like any other, a tangled tale of achievements and victories, disappointments and rejections, love, and family. His donation of a lifeboat to the Isle of Man represented the final act of a long and eventful life.

John's naval career was something in which he took great pride, but it also became a source of personal frustration and resentment. The Royal Navy was far more meritocratic than the British Army at the time, but the likelihood of promotion to the upper ranks was regularly improved by connections and influence, dependent on relationships that John lacked but sought to nurture. He found himself forced to battle the Admiralty just as he had battled the French, Dutch and Danish.

When Commander Monk died, he was buried in the churchyard of St Helen and Mary in Neston on the Wirral. He and his family lie beneath three large stone slabs, laid flat on the ground. The 140 years since his death have not been kind to his resting place. The weather has worn away at the letters engraved into the porous sandstone, leaving the family graves largely unmarked, and several years ago a nearby tree was toppled by a storm, knocking off a commemorative brass plaque.

I have written this in his honour. During his lifetime, he enjoyed regaling people with tales of his adventures and, having got to know him over the last few years, I feel sure that he would appreciate taking centre stage again. He might even grumble that it was long overdue.

Simon Francis Brown
February 2023

Prologue. The Irish Sea, October 1889

A violent storm had raged in the Irish Sea throughout one Sunday night in October 1889, and fierce winds had whipped the waters around the Isle of Man into mountainous waves. As daylight broke, onlookers on the hills around the town of Peel spied a stricken merchant ship at the mercy of the continuing storm, her masts and rigging carried overboard. Even from a distance, it seemed that anyone still on board faced certain death. The town lay on the west coast of the island, a lee shore in the prevailing winds. Either the ship would break up and sink at sea, or she would be driven onshore by the wind and waves and smash against the rocky coast. Hopes were briefly raised when a large steamer appeared to approach her but then faded as the steamer continued southward, perhaps deciding that to provide assistance in such conditions would be impossible.

That morning, a crowd gathered in Peel's harbour with a mixture of dread and anticipation. All eyes were on the harbourmaster as he announced his decision to attempt a rescue. Peel had a new lifeboat station, which housed the *John Monk*, a thirty-seven foot, twelve-oared self-righter, received four years earlier after a private bequest from an old naval captain. The coxswain selected a crew of volunteers for what each man knew would be a cold and potentially deadly rescue attempt. The crowd watched as the twelve men from the town, their husbands, brothers, sons and friends, donned their cork life jackets, left the safety of land and began to row their small boat out into the angry sea...[1]

1. A childhood in Parkgate

John Monk was born on the Wirral in the late summer of 1791, the seventh surviving child of Parkgate customs officer, William Monk, and his wife Esther Matthews. Esther's family had been a part of the local community for at least a century, and several generations of her ancestors lay in the family plot beside the church of St Mary and St Helen. The Matthews of Parkgate had a long and proud maritime heritage, one that John and several of his brothers would each continue.

It was only natural that the men of the family would turn so often to the water in search of employment. The Wirral peninsula forms the westernmost point of Cheshire, with Liverpool to the North and Wales to the South. The Irish Sea lies to the west, and the two estuaries of the Dee and the Mersey flank it on either side. The picturesque village of Parkgate lies on its southern bank.

The River Dee had been a commercial waterway for thousands of years, and the Romans had operated a port at Chester, twelve miles further upstream. Each day, as the tide rose in the estuary, all manner of merchant vessels and fishing boats approached the Parkgate shore, and as the water receded, natural patterns of sand, mud, gullies, channels and vegetation were exposed across the flats out towards the main river channel. It made for a dramatic landscape, with big skies and long, uninterrupted views of the Welsh hills. Beyond the distant seaward horizon lay the Isle of Man, and beyond that Ireland and the

Atlantic. The estuary was central to the life of the community, providing food, transport and identity.

Esther's grandfather had been a shipbuilder, and her father John Matthews (1708-1799) was for many years master of the *Minerva*, a merchant brig sailing between Dublin and Parkgate as regularly as temperamental tides, winds and weather would allow. In contrast to many of his peers, Matthews had built a reputation as a man to be trusted. Arranging for an acquaintance to visit Dublin in 1752, Dr Patrick Delany wrote in a letter, 'I will appoint the best vessel upon the coast, the *Minerva*, with the civilest and soberest master, Capt. Mathews, to meet you... and convey you hither.'[1] For the master of a merchantman to be sober was clearly not something one could take for granted.

John Matthew's first wife, Catharine Pemberton (1716-1744), had died during childbirth, leaving him alone with two daughters and a son. Six years later, he remarried, this time to Elisabeth Rothery (1725-1807), but even civil and sober ships' captains are not immune to family scandal. Elisabeth was a full seventeen years her new husband's junior and had a younger sister, Sarah, much closer in age to her husband's son Joseph. To John's horror, romance blossomed between son and sister-in-law, and the two married and moved away to Liverpool, with Joseph ignoring his furious father's threats to disown him. John Matthews and Elisabeth had six children together. Esther, John Monk's mother, was the baby of the family, born on September 2nd, 1759.

John's Monk's father, William, had no such nautical roots. The Monks hailed from Chester, where they had long been involved in the newspaper and printing business. His grandfather, Roger Adams (1661-1741), had been a successful printer and bookseller. He was also the original proprietor of a local newspaper, which first appeared in 1730 as *Adams's Weekly Courant*, and it was at Roger's printworks in New Gate Street that his daughter Dorothy (1719-1757) fell for a young apprentice, William Monk (1718-1758). William and Dorothy married and later took over the printing and newspaper business after her father's death. Among their children were twin boys, William and Benjamin, born in Chester on November 20th, 1753. The family business was destined for their eldest brother, so William and Benjamin knew they would have to choose their own paths. The two boys each took posts with the customs service and in December 1775, aged 23, William was appointed as a junior officer at Parkgate, the small port on the south Wirral shore, where his brother Benjamin joined him.[2]

The service from Parkgate to Dublin was one of the principal routes for passengers and post travelling between England and Ireland during the eighteenth century, and it gave the little village an unlikely role of national significance. The port also marked the uppermost point at which the Dee estuary was navigable to larger vessels, so cargo destined for Chester had to complete its journey either by carriage or smaller boat. As the Parkgate anchorage grew in popularity, money and development followed until, by the time of William and Benjamin's arrival in 1775, the village had been transformed from sleepy hamlet into a seafront of attractive Georgian buildings, including lodging houses and taverns like the George Inn, each ready to house, feed and entertain passengers waiting to continue their journeys.

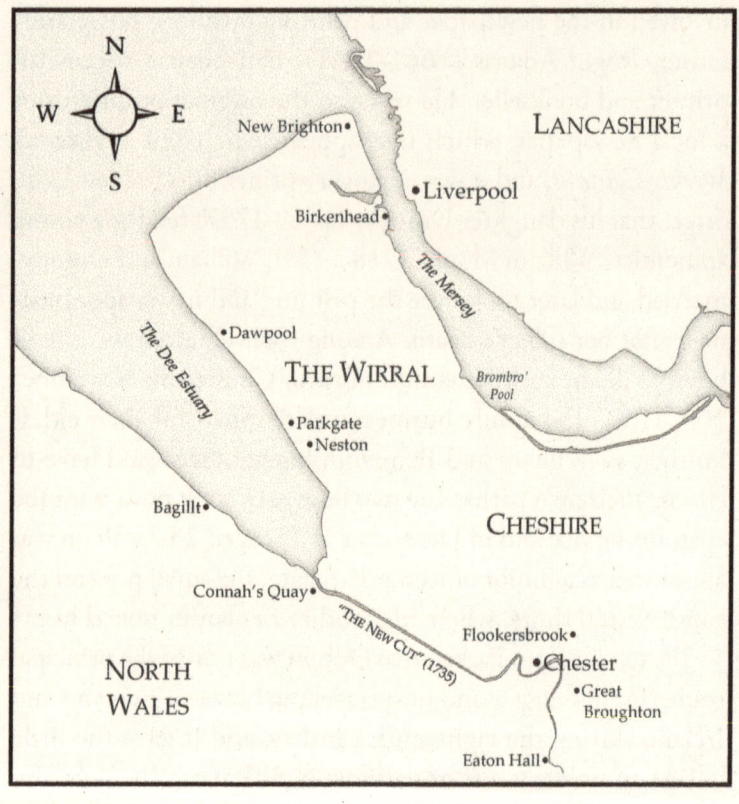

Four years after William's arrival in the village as a young customs officer, he and Esther Matthews married in neighbouring Neston in 1779. They made their home in Parkgate, close to the rest of the Matthews clan and a short walk from William's job at the custom house.

William and brother Benjamin were junior officers in a full-time team of seven. Benjamin was a tidewaiter and William was a landwaiter, archaic titles that bear describing. Parkgate had no jetty or sea wall at this time, so arriving vessels anchored about a hundred yards out in the estuary, from where cargo and passengers were off-loaded into smaller boats and rowed ashore. As the tidewaiter, Benjamin was the first customs official to board a vessel as she arrived at the anchorage. He would prepare a list of all the cargo to be discharged, and make sure that nothing was off-loaded unofficially. When compiled, he would provide his list to William. As the landwaiter, William remained on the quayside to tick off everything as it reached the shore. Together the brothers would check that both their records tallied and that nothing had been smuggled over the side while their backs were turned.

William and Esther had eleven children together, nine of whom reached adulthood. Elizabeth was the eldest, born in 1779, two years before Charles (1781), then William (1782), the twins Esther and Ann who died as infants (1784), then came Joseph in 1786, Arabella in 1788 and a second Ann in 1789. John, the subject of our story, was the ninth child, born in the late summer of 1791 on September 1st, before a younger brother called Whitehouse (1795) and finally another Esther, known as 'Nessie' (1798), with whom John would live for over twenty years in his retirement. The children also had cousins nearby. Their uncle Benjamin and his wife Elizabeth, who had also set up home in Parkgate, had children of their own, among them Richard, Maria and Edward.

Walking from his family's home down to the waterfront, the young John may have watched as wealthy passengers and government officials arrived by coach in Parkgate from across the country, impatient to continue their onward journey to Dublin, and prepared to board the two-masted sailing vessels anchored in the estuary. As well as the passengers being rowed out in small boats, he would have witnessed the noise and activity as freight, such as cattle and coal, was loaded, ready to sail. He would have seen vessels arrive, sometimes carrying poor Irish emigrants hoping to find seasonal work. In the middle of it all would have been his father and uncle, busily making sure that paperwork and cargo lists were all in order.

Particularly during the warmer months, John would have seen tourists arrive, drawn to one of the country's earliest seaside resorts, although distinctly quaint by today's standards. Sea bathing had grown in popularity nationwide since the middle of the eighteenth century, as doctors and the medical establishment promoted the health benefits of saltwater and fresh sea air. Parkgate was well placed to benefit from this, being a spot of natural beauty, with fine sand, sea breezes and views across the estuary.

The Monk children were born into the early decades of the Industrial Revolution, and many of the era's greatest innovations were originating from close to home in the north of England. The first modern factory appeared in Derbyshire in 1771, operating both day and night. The first iron bridge was erected in Shropshire in 1779, and by 1800 a network of canals had spread from the north-west to criss-cross the country. For all the innovations on land, transport by sea was still in the age of sail. The first steam vessels emerged in the 1780s, but early examples were small and inefficient, suited only to use on canals and rivers. It would take several decades and a string of technical advances before steamships could challenge the superiority of sail on the world's oceans.

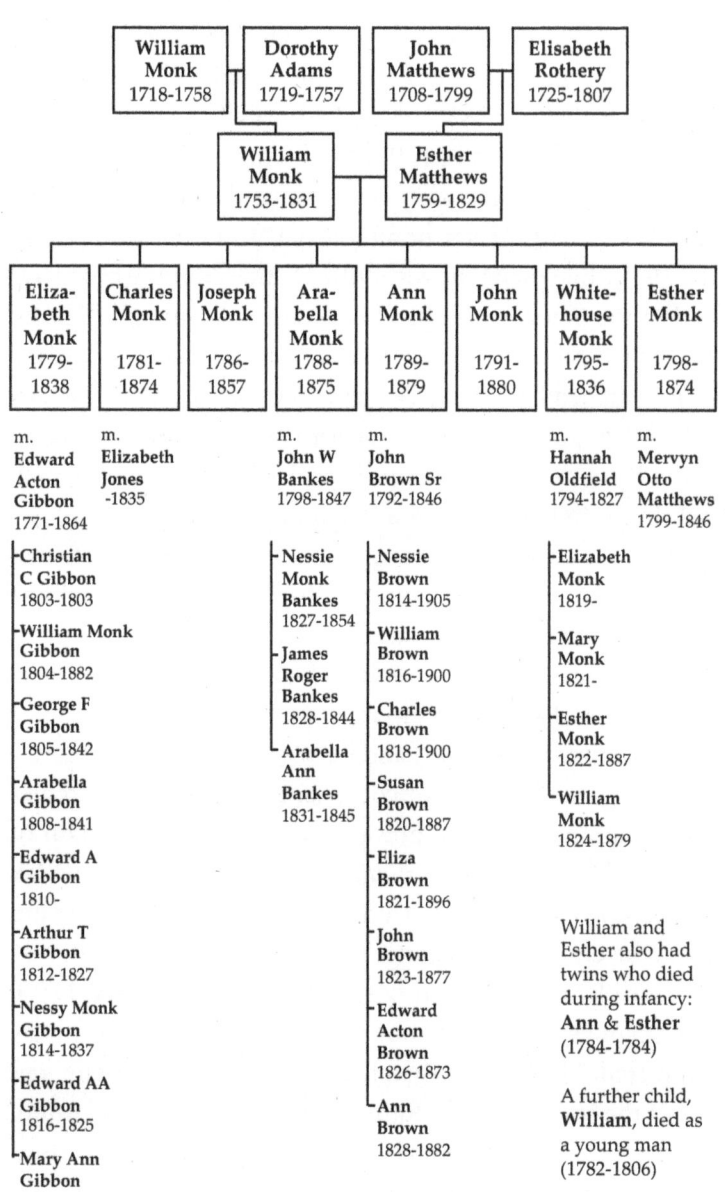

| William Monk 1718-1758 | Dorothy Adams 1719-1757 | John Matthews 1708-1799 | Elisabeth Rothery 1725-1807 |

William Monk 1753-1831 — Esther Matthews 1759-1829

| Eliza-beth Monk 1779-1838 | Charles Monk 1781-1874 | Joseph Monk 1786-1857 | Ara-bella Monk 1788-1875 | Ann Monk 1789-1879 | John Monk 1791-1880 | White-house Monk 1795-1836 | Esther Monk 1798-1874 |

m.
Edward
Acton
Gibbon
1771-1864

m.
Elizabeth
Jones
-1835

m.
John W
Bankes
1798-1847

m.
John
Brown Sr
1792-1846

m.
Hannah
Oldfield
1794-1827

m.
Mervyn
Otto
Matthews
1799-1846

-Christian
C Gibbon
1803-1803

-William Monk
Gibbon
1804-1882

-George F
Gibbon
1805-1842

-Arabella
Gibbon
1808-1841

-Edward A
Gibbon
1810-

-Arthur T
Gibbon
1812-1827

-Nessy Monk
Gibbon
1814-1837

-Edward AA
Gibbon
1816-1825

-Mary Ann
Gibbon
1816-1836

-Nessie
Monk
Bankes
1827-1854

-James
Roger
Bankes
1828-1844

-Arabella
Ann
Bankes
1831-1845

-Nessie
Brown
1814-1905

-William
Brown
1816-1900

-Charles
Brown
1818-1900

-Susan
Brown
1820-1887

-Eliza
Brown
1821-1896

-John
Brown
1823-1877

-Edward
Acton
Brown
1826-1873

-Ann
Brown
1828-1882

-Elizabeth
Monk
1819-

-Mary
Monk
1821-

-Esther
Monk
1822-1887

-William
Monk
1824-1879

William and
Esther also had
twins who died
during infancy:
Ann & Esther
(1784-1784)

A further child,
William, died as
a young man
(1782-1806)

Beyond Britain's shores, however, the world seemed to be consumed by unrest and upheaval. The American Revolutionary War had ended in 1783 and the Irish rebellion against British rule had been crushed in 1798. Most worryingly, to the south-east, France had been in turmoil since the storming of the Bastille in 1789. At her home on the Wirral in the summer of 1791, while pregnant with John, Esther Monk would have read in the Chester newspapers about the attempted flight of the French royal family from Paris. Over the next two years, as she watched her young son grow and take his first steps, she would have followed with concern as guillotines were set up in the Place de la Révolution, King Louis XVI was executed, and the period known as the Reign of Terror began.

Amid the chaos consuming France in the 1790s, a talented Corsican officer named Napoleon Bonaparte rose through the ranks of the French army and, after his campaign in Egypt, the young general seized power on his return to Paris in 1799. Bonaparte was a popular and intelligent politician, as well as a brilliant military strategist, and he began to stabilise a country previously on the brink of collapse. For the old monarchies like Britain and Austria, however, the rise and expansion of the French Republic, or rather the revolutionary ideals which underpinned it, represented a threat to their very existence and had to be crushed at all costs.

France had been at war with most of Europe since 1793. Her enemies changed throughout the years as nations were conquered, liberated or switched allegiances, but Britain was one of the few constants. Ranged against the French in 1806, when John joined the Royal Navy, were the nations of the Third Coalition, among them Russia, Austria and Britain.

Bonaparte was now Emperor Napoleon I. His empire was huge, and French influence extended across large parts of continental Europe. To date, though, any attempts by Bonaparte to invade Britain had been unsuccessful. The English Channel was barely twenty miles wide at its narrowest but presented Bonaparte with a formidable challenge. Britain's land defences were increasingly strong, and its navy was growing ever larger. The nation's confidence in its defences is nicely illustrated by Lord St Vincent's quip to the Board of Admiralty in 1801: 'I do not say, my Lords, that the French can not come – I only say that they cannot come by sea.'[3]

After the collapse of the Peace of Amiens in 1803, Napoleon redoubled his efforts. Flush with funds from the sale of Louisiana to the Americans, the French assembled an army of 200,000 men along the coast between Boulogne and Bruges and built a flotilla of small invasion barges. The plan began to fall apart in 1804 when a large-scale test of the barges went disastrously wrong due to bad weather. Worse was to come for Bonaparte. His attempt in July 1805 to distract the British fleet away from the Channel ended in failure at the Battle of Cape Finisterre, and this was followed just months later by the crushing defeat of the Franco-Spanish fleet at the Battle of Trafalgar on October 21st.

Bonaparte's failures were lampooned by London's newspapers but behind the bravado, the spectre of Old Boney, so close across the narrow Channel, continued to strike fear into many British hearts.

2. Volunteer, first-class

Many years later, with the war long since concluded and his years as a mariner behind him, John Monk sat at his desk to write a summary of his naval career. He prepared several such accounts over the years, usually for presentation to influential contacts whom he hoped might assist in his quest for promotion. The tone can often be rather blunt and unpolished, and details are occasionally muddled. On this particular day, as John began to write, his memory seemed to be failing him...

I am afraid I can't give the dates and particulars of my services in the late war not having been employed in the Royal Navy since 1817, but, to the best of my recollection, I will do my best. I entered the services in 1806, onboard the Dictator *64, Captain James Macnamara, North Sea station...*[1]

Those seas of the world where Britain had influence were organised by the Royal Navy into naval commands, known as stations. Each had its commander-in-chief, with a fleet or a smaller squadron of ships and one or more naval bases from which to control operations. John's years of active service from 1806 to 1816 would take him through most of Europe's stations, from the North Sea to the Channel, north to the Baltic and south to the Mediterranean.

John was a boy of 14 when he arrived in Great Yarmouth in July 1806, ready to enter His Majesty King George III's Navy as a volunteer, first-class, a rating given to young gentlemen with aspirations of officer rank, prior to their appointment as midshipman. The long journey across England to meet his new captain and shipmates would have taken several days by carriage, two hundred bumpy miles east from the Wirral to the Norfolk coast. His first ship, the sixty-four-gun HMS *Dictator*, lay offshore in Yarmouth Roads, back from North Sea duty to reprovision and for general maintenance.

After twenty years of service and the tough conditions in the North Sea, it took an increasing amount of work to keep the old *Dictator* seaworthy. She had been launched in Limehouse in 1783 and had seen action at the Reduction of Trinidad in 1797 and as a troopship at the Battle of Aboukir in 1801,[2] but by the time John stepped onto her deck in 1806, she was showing her age. North Sea duty meant rough seas, heavy winds and often violent storms, and records show that it was becoming a constant struggle for the carpenter, caulkers and the rest of the ship's company to keep the old wooden hull watertight. As the waves and wind threw the creaking ship from side to side, the wood twisted, expanded and shrunk, and gaps were forced open between the planks. Each time the *Dictator* returned to the Yarmouth Roads anchorage, large teams of caulkers came on board and worked their way through each deck, filling cracks with a mix of tar and old rope fibres, known as oakum. Repairs to the hull itself would have to wait until the ship was next out of the water.

The *Dictator* was classed as a third-rate ship of the line.[3] All ships in the Royal Navy were given a rating based on the number of guns they carried. A first-rate ship was one with more than one hundred guns, the most famous today being

HMS *Victory*. These were huge beasts, about 220 feet long and manned by a ship's company of over eight hundred men. They could fire the most powerful broadside in a large fleet battle, but they were also heavy and slow-moving, and could often be found on blockade duty. Second-rate ships were those with more than ninety guns, and a third-rate such as HMS *Dictator,* John's floating home for the next two years, carried at least sixty-four guns and typically required a ship's company of between 500 and 650 men. They balanced speed and power and were also more manoeuvrable than some of their larger cousins. The number of guns is a useful, if unreliable, guide to a ship's size and is typically shown in brackets after the name.

Preparing an account of a junior officer's naval career is a tricky undertaking. Published accounts of the war, in common with contemporary newspaper reports of individual engagements, often name only a ship's captain, and the story of one man's day-to-day existence at sea quickly gets absorbed into that of his ship, as several hundred men become one unit operating their giant, creaking machine of wood, iron and canvas.

The ADM papers at The National Archives at Kew provide a resource of remarkable depth and breadth, and allow a researcher to build a more detailed profile of an officer, but the logs, letters, rolls and records demand patience and dedication in return. Among them, the captains' logs detail the daily movements of each one of the ships on which John served, and include notes of key events on board. There are also captains' letters, dispatches and personal communications from this period, in which John himself appears, either centre stage or as a fleeting glimpse.

Viewed in the round, the different sources paint a picture of an eager young officer, doing all the right things as he seeks to get ahead. He volunteers for boat actions and operations on shore, he shows loyalty to each of his captains, and he speaks in terms of honour and glory. The right attitude would take John so far, but his eventual progression through the ranks of the Royal Navy would also depend on opportunity, connections and a fair amount of good fortune.

John's captain on the *Dictator* was an Irishman, James Macnamara, and, unusually, his log for the morning mentions John's arrival on board:

Yarmo'. Sunday 6ᵗʰ July 1806. Moderate breezes and hazy weather, employed occasionally. Received 672 lbs fresh beef, sent up topgallant yards, carpenters making chocks for the rudder, caulkers caulking the main deck, hazy with thick rain, joined Mr John Monk, Midshipman.[4]

Macnamara was mistaken in his record, as it would be several months before John was officially appointed midshipman. For these first few months, the *Dictator's* muster book shows him listed as an able seaman, or A.B.. To join the Navy at fourteen was common for young men with aspirations of officer status, as it allowed them to build up enough sea time and practical experience to sit the lieutenant's examination. Passing for lieutenant generally required the candidate to have spent six years at sea and to appear to be at least twenty years old, although these criteria were not always followed.

John had barely a week to accustom himself to the rules and routines of his new home before the ship received her final supply of provisions and was made ready for sea. On July 13th, she weighed anchor and sailed eastwards with other ships of the fleet. There was a light breeze and constant rain, as there would be for much of the coming months. The squadron made a short patrol of the sea off the northern Dutch coast and returned to Yarmouth just a week later. John had been given a drizzly but gentle introduction to the war.

The French had occupied Holland since 1795, but earlier that month Napoleon had appointed his third brother, Louis Napoleon (1778–1846), as the new King of Holland. He would prove to be quite a popular king, although not with his brother, who criticized Louis for showing loyalty to his Dutch subjects above France.[5] For the rest of the summer and autumn, John and the *Dictator* repeated this familiar pattern of short patrols off the Dutch coast, with frequent visits in and out of Yarmouth Roads to reprovision.

Patrols or 'cruises' such as these provided a visible presence to the enemy, but they were also hunting trips. Royal Navy ships boarded and interrogated each ship, brig or sloop they encountered, searching for enemy vessels that might be taken as prizes. At times, the pattern of spot, chase, board and interrogate was daily.

The prize system was central to the economic warfare that was waged during the costly and protracted conflict, and strict protocols governed whether and how a prize could be taken. The High Court of Admiralty held prize courts, to which all prize claims had to be presented, to deal with questions of piracy and to ensure the proper distribution of legitimate spoils. Each time Macnamara sent the boats of the *Dictator* to board an unfamiliar vessel, his men were required to inspect all the ship's papers to establish its nationality. Most would produce friendly or neutral paperwork and be allowed to continue on their way, but others might be French or Dutch and could be taken as prizes. A bundle of papers for each of these prize claims is still held today at The National Archives, each neatly tied with a ribbon two hundred years ago and each a snapshot of maritime life at the time. The High Court of Admiralty would also pay 'head money' for seamen taken from an enemy ship. Captured men could look forward nervously either to a long stay in prison or a return to their homeland as part of a prisoner exchange.

Seamen in the Royal Navy were notoriously badly paid, and prize money could provide a welcome bonus, although the ratios of division were a perennial cause of disgruntlement. Still an able seaman, John's portion of any prize money would have been very small indeed. The distribution was revised in 1808 but the largest part still went to the senior ranks. A quarter of the value went to the captain, one eighth to the officers, one eighth to warrant officers and midshipmen, and a half was divided between petty officers and several hundred seamen.

John got his first glimpse of a prize in the late afternoon of September 5th, when the British ships spied several unidentified sails. After successfully giving chase, a party from the *Dictator* boarded a Dutch two-masted dogger, the *Vrouw Sophia*, bound for Rotterdam laden with herring.[6] The crew of eight were brought on board, and Macnamara ordered two of his officers and six men to deliver the potential prize to Yarmouth.

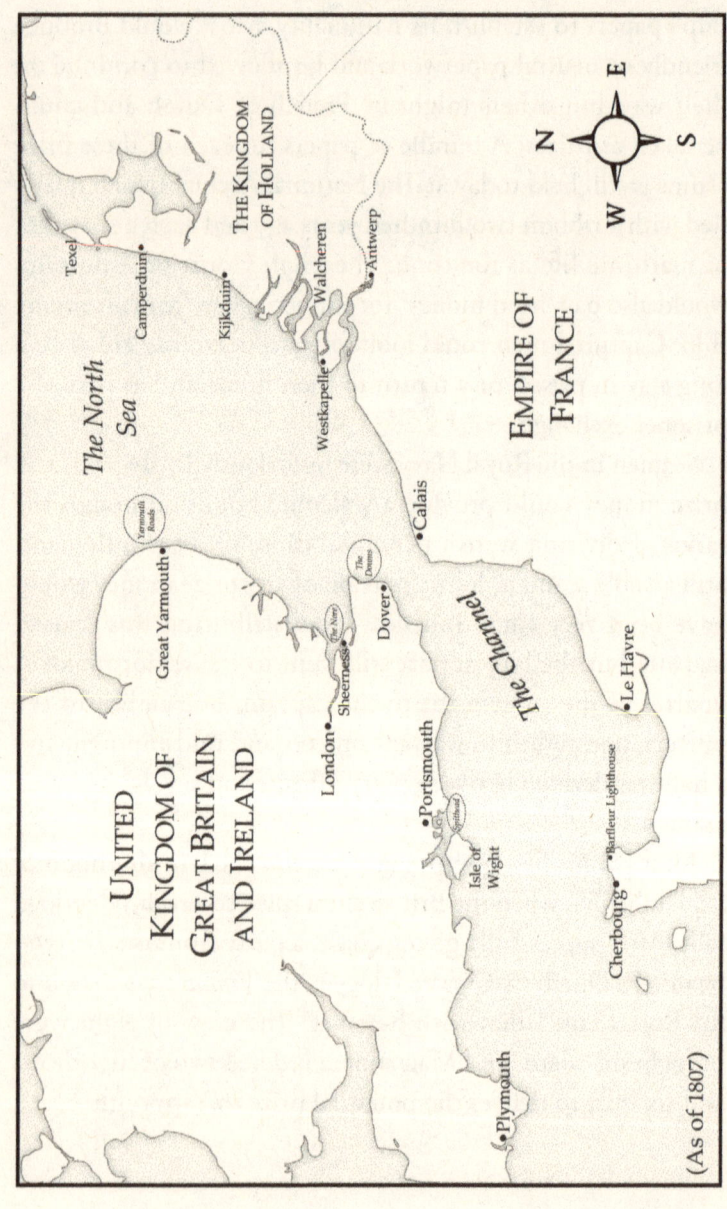

THE KINGDOM OF HOLLAND

Texel

Camperduin

Kijkduin

Walcheren

Antwerp

Westkapelle

EMPIRE OF FRANCE

The North Sea

Calais

N E S W

Yarmouth Roads

The Downs

Great Yarmouth

The Nore

Dover

Le Havre

Sheerness

London

The Channel

UNITED KINGDOM OF GREAT BRITAIN AND IRELAND

Portsmouth

Barfleur Lighthouse

Spithead

Isle of Wight

Cherbourg

Plymouth

(As of 1807)

Life on board the *Dictator* would have been unlike anything the young John had experienced. Within her wooden hull, just 159 feet long and forty-four feet wide, lived six hundred men, all required to operate as a single unit. Macnamara was the all-powerful captain. He had five lieutenants, numbered as per their seniority, the most senior being the first lieutenant, the captain's second-in-command. Below them were the warrant officers, such as the master, surgeon, purser and carpenter, and the petty officers, among them the skilled craftsmen tasked with keeping the ship in good condition - the armourer, ropemaker, sailmaker and caulker, each with one or more assistants, or mates - and up to fifteen midshipmen.

There were several hundred seamen, the more experienced known as able seamen, others as ordinary. Both groups looked down on landsmen, those inexperienced men likely on their first ship, good only for moving barrels and scrubbing decks. There were also ship's boys, children as young as 8 or 9, who were used for all manner of menial jobs and acted as 'powder monkeys' during battle, carrying gunpowder to the gun crews. Separate to the seamen were the armed marines, soldiers rather than sailors, their separateness accentuated by their distinctive red jackets. They were useful in times of battle, but they were on hand more generally to enforce order among the ship's crew. Even then, the ship's company was not yet complete. The captain and principal warrant officers each had their servants and the captain a cook of his own.

Every man's routine was governed by the ship's bell and the bosun's call. The bell was struck every half an hour, day and night, timed with a thirty-minute hourglass. A watch lasted eight bells, or four hours, with shorter 'dog watches' in the early evening, which varied the schedule for officers on watch and allowed all men to eat a hot evening meal. The high-pitched whistle known as the bosun's call carried commands audibly through the large ship, even in rough weather.

After serving his first few months on board HMS *Dictator* as an able seaman, John was formally promoted to midshipman in November 1806, perhaps when he had proved himself worthy of Macnamara's initial support.

John was now a senior petty officer, also known as a cockpit officer, after the area towards the stern of the ship, where he and his fellow 'middies' ate and slept. Some would have been boys of John's age or younger, often from wealthy or well-connected families, learning the ropes and being taught how to act as naval officers and young gentlemen. Other midshipmen were older, unable or unwilling to climb the ladder of promotion.

As a midshipman, John's main role was to help the lieutenants control the ship. It was considerable responsibility for a young man. He could be called on to take watches on deck or to command groups of sailors on particular tasks. He might even be given command of a captured prize or ordered to lead a ship's boat in a landing or cutting-out expedition, each an opportunity to demonstrate bravery and zeal, highly prized qualities in the Georgian Navy.

Alongside the practical training and first-hand experience of responsibility, John and the other midshipmen also spent time with the ship's schoolmaster, being educated in seamanship and the complicated mathematics of navigation, astronomy, and trigonometry. There would be hard work ahead, but the post showed John a path through to the commissioned officer rank of lieutenant, if he stayed healthy and if fortune was on his side.

Not all of the seamen under midshipman John's command, as they scrubbed the deck or tarred the rigging, were there by choice. Many were volunteers, tempted by regular meals and steady employment, but others were there through force, taken against their will under the British system of impressment. There were two types of impressment, hot and cold, and both could be legalised in times of war. In a cold press, naval ships positioned themselves in the centre of shipping lanes and held up inbound ocean-going merchantmen. The merchant master was informed that so many hands were required. If enough volunteered, then the merchantman could continue but, if not, men would be taken regardless. In a hot press, a press gang would sweep unannounced through a coastal town or city, looking for experienced mariners anywhere it might find them.

One of the most striking observations from a review of the captain's logs, whether of the *Dictator* or others of John's ships, is that on the majority of days, nothing noteworthy happens. For each day on which the guns are fired in anger or on which an enemy vessel is boarded, there are many, many more days spent scrubbing decks, painting the hull or transferring heavy barrels of water and provisions from supply vessels. The ship's company could look forward to long periods of boredom punctuated by moments of sheer terror, as the adage goes.

The irascible Captain Macnamara

Quite how John had secured his appointment on James Macnamara's ship is not known, but it is rare to find a midshipman's arrival noted in the captain's log, which lends credence to the idea of a family relationship. This was quite common. Upper- and middle-class families regularly used whatever personal connections they could muster to advance their son or nephew's career. A captain appointed his midshipmen and was routinely encouraged by relatives and friends to find an opening for their offspring. In John's case, it may have been connected to his new captain's Irish roots.

Macnamara came from a family with a strong naval background. His father Michael had been born in Dublin in about 1730 and would have been a contemporary of John's grandfather, John Matthews, who was well known in the city as the master of the *Minerva*. Both men had died in the previous decade, but a family connection may have been one the Monks could use. Macnamara would himself have passed through Parkgate on occasion when travelling between Ireland and England. Alternatively, the connection may have been through Edward Acton Gibbon, who had married John's eldest sister, Elizabeth, in 1802. Edward had been born in the small village of Sleedagh in County Wexford,[7] just fifteen miles from the even smaller village of Redgate, the birthplace of Macnamara's mother Bridget Waters.[8] Edward was a shipping agent at the time and well connected within the Dublin maritime community. He showed in later years that he was always keen to advance John's situation.

John's future would be closely linked to that of his charismatic new captain, and he showed loyalty to Macnamara throughout his time in the Navy, following him first from HMS *Dictator* to the *Edgar* and then on to the *Berwick*. Macnamara was an experienced, if irascible, captain and would prove to be a true and consistent mentor to John in the coming years. In a system of promotion that could be influenced by the support of more senior, well-connected figures, Macnamara was the closest John would have to a patron, as he sought, with the enthusiasm of youth, to make his way through the ranks.

Macnamara had had a long and well-regarded career by this point, and had served with prominent naval officers like Hood, Jervis, and his personal friend, Horatio Nelson. He had been promoted to master and commander in 1793 and had made a name for himself as an accomplished frigate captain. He had served on HMS *Victory* during the French Revolutionary Wars and had already served in both the East and West Indies and the Mediterranean. He had developed a reputation through the years for bravery with a hint of recklessness.

A family portrait shows Macnamara with an impressive head of tight curls and a prominent nose. In his prime, he was a 'strong, bold and active man', although he was likely described less kindly by some of his crew.[9] He could be a brutal disciplinarian, with a fierce temper, easily roused. Like his ship, though, Macnamara was beginning to show signs of his age. The next eight years would take their toll on him, and ill-health would eventually force him out of the service.

The quick temper and bellicose manner that had made Macnamara a captain to be feared at sea could sometimes cause him problems on land. For all his years' service to his country, James Macnamara is perhaps best known today for his part in a fatal duel, three years before John Monk first boarded his ship. It followed something as trivial as an argument about his dog…

It was a spring morning in London in 1803, and Macnamara was on leave during the Peace of Amiens. He was riding in Hyde

Park with a group of friends when his dog, Lion, began to fight with another, belonging to Colonel Robert Montgomery. The dogs resolved their differences, but an argument erupted between the two owners. Versions of the dispute were recounted several times during the subsequent trial and ran broadly as follows:[10]

MONTGOMERY: Whose dog is this?

MACNAMARA: It is my dog.

MONTGOMERY, curtly: If you do not call your dog off, I shall knock him down.

MACNAMARA: Have you the arrogance to say you will knock my dog down? How is it possible to prevent the fighting of dogs in an open field?

MONTGOMERY: Sir, it is not my intention to quarrel with you, but if your dog falls upon mine, I shall knock him down.

MACNAMARA: Sir, if you knock my dog down you must knock me down also.

The two groups parted, with Macnamara angrily shaking his stick towards Montgomery as they left the park. They met again shortly after in Piccadilly, where further angry words were spoken.

MONTGOMERY: Why did you not dismount and take your dog away?

MACNAMARA: I am an officer in his Majesty's Navy and unaccustomed to such arrogant language.

MONTGOMERY, handing over his address card: Sir, if you conceive yourself injured you know where I live. You ought to take care of your dog.

MACNAMARA: I shall do that without your permission.

Once the challenge had been made, Macnamara felt honour-bound to accept. Plans were made for a duel that evening and, at dusk, the two men and their seconds climbed Primrose Hill. A servant followed, carrying a box of pistols. On reaching the top of the hill, Macnamara and Montgomery took their weapons. Each took twelve paces, turned to face one another, and fired. Macnamara was wounded but remained on his feet. Colonel Montgomery fell, groaning, and died a few minutes later.

Macnamara was arrested and charged with manslaughter. Lord Nelson visited his friend before the trial and was clearly of the view that Montgomery's dog was to blame, as he shared in a typically untidy letter:

My Dear Mac, … If your antagonist had not fell at this moment, his damn'd dog would have brought him into a scrape. I have heard more on that subject than is necessary to put on paper but all in your favour. [11]

Nelson's letter ends with a poignant footnote, 'I hope we shall fight the French together yet', something which was not to be. Captain Mac would take charge of his next ship, the *Dictator*, in June 1805 and was serving in the North Sea when his friend was killed by a sniper's bullet at Cape Trafalgar, off the coast of Spain that October.

The case against Macnamara was heard on April 20th, 1803, at the Old Bailey. He spoke eloquently and forcefully in his own defence, addressing the jury seated due to pain from his wound. He argued that although the subject of the initial argument had been trivial, had he walked away from Montgomery's challenge, he would have shown weakness and his authority as a captain would have been undermined:

Gentlemen, I am a captain in the British Navy. My character you can hear only from others; but to maintain any character in that station I must be respected. When called upon to lead others into honourable danger, I must not be supposed to be a man who had sought safety by submitting to what custom has taught others to consider a disgrace... Gentlemen, I submit myself entirely to your judgment. I hope to obtain my liberty, through your verdict, and to employ it with honour in the defence of the liberties of my country.

Macnamara's trump card was his friendship with Lord Nelson. Two years before his final, defining victory at the Battle of Trafalgar, Nelson was already a national hero. He took the stand and spoke of Macnamara's good character and peaceful nature:

I have known Captain Macnamara nine years; he has been at various times under my command. During my acquaintance with him, I had not only the highest esteem and respect for him as an officer, but I always looked upon him as a gentleman, who would not take an affront from any man; yet, as I stand here before God and my country, I never knew nor heard that he ever gave offence to man, woman or child during my acquaintance with him.

Macnamara's defence had offered nothing to challenge the facts of the case but had formed a stirring war cry of honour, respect and national liberty. With passions roused, the members of the jury declared Macnamara to be Not Guilty. He was a free man and would be able to return to battle, should the increasingly fragile peace with France fail to hold.

Whether the younger John, as a child of twelve in Parkgate, happened to have read the newspaper coverage of his future captain's trial in 1803 is not recorded, but, along with his fellow midshipmen on the *Dictator* and every man among the ship's company, John would have known of the incident, and would have been left in no doubt that his captain was not a man to be crossed.

The Bombardment of Copenhagen, 1807

John had been on HMS *Dictator* for less than a year when his captain informed his officers in the spring of 1807 that he had received a new posting, to HMS *Edgar*, also a third-rate but larger, with seventy-four guns compared to the *Dictator*'s sixty-four. The implications for John would have been uncertain. It was common practice for a captain to take several of his officers and seamen with him onto a new ship. In return for their loyalty, the captain would look for opportunities to advance these junior officers' careers. As John may have hoped, Macnamara promptly wrote to the Admiralty to ask that he and several others of the *Dictator*'s midshipmen be allowed to join their captain on the *Edgar*:

The undernamed petty officers, midshipmen belonging to HMS Dictator, *having no other friend in the service but myself, I have to request… their discharge into the* Edgar. (June 10th, 1807, London)[12]

The Admiralty approved his request in part and three of Macnamara's eight named midshipmen were discharged immediately to the *Edgar*. John was not one of them, though, and it would be almost a year before he and the remaining four joined them, despite Macnamara's regular entreaties to his superiors.

The new captain on the *Dictator* was Donald Campbell, and in just the same way as Macnamara had sought to do, Campbell brought with him several of his own midshipmen, young men he already knew and trusted. As Macnamara had phrased it in his request to the Admiralty, John had been separated from his one friend in the service. He would need to make a new friend and gain a new captain's confidence all over again.

As a young midshipman, John Monk would not have been privy to Admiralty discussions in July 1807, as the *Dictator* lay at anchor in Yarmouth Roads, but he would have seen clear signs that something was afoot. Several large ships appeared from the west on July 20th and a string of admirals began to arrive, among them the commander of the Channel fleet himself, Admiral James Gambier, who hoisted his flag on the *Prince of Wales* (98).

By the time the order was received to set sail on July 26th, the fleet in Yarmouth Roads comprised sixteen ships of the line, six frigates and a large number of brigs, bomb ships, lighters and merchant vessels requisitioned as transports. The sky was overcast and the air was hazy, but the fleet would have made for an impressive sight, nonetheless.

The destination was Copenhagen, capital of Denmark-Norway, one of the very few nations still doggedly asserting its neutrality.[13] John's first large-scale engagement was to be one of the most controversial of the whole war.

Denmark's neutral stance was pragmatic. To side openly with either France or Britain in the conflict would make an immediate enemy of the other. By 1807, though, this position was looking increasingly untenable, and Danish forces were gathered in the south of the country to protect against French attack. British fears were two-fold. If Bonaparte were to gain control of the large Danish navy, either through force or diplomacy, it could be used to launch an invasion of Britain's shores. The other priority was to maintain access to the Baltic Sea, a critical source of naval supplies, primarily the specialist wood needed for masts, hulls and other parts of a wooden sailing fleet. Baltic states also provided vital trading revenue, as Britain struggled to avoid bankruptcy during the hugely expensive war.

In the British government's eyes, the risks were too great to ignore. The fleet was sailing north from Yarmouth to present an offer to the Danes, but an offer that was not to be declined.

Denmark sits as the gateway to the Baltic. Sweden lies to the east, Norway to the north, and the Jutland peninsula, the country's greatest land mass, is bounded by the north German states to the south. The capital city of Copenhagen lies on the eastern coast of Zealand, the largest of the country's four hundred islands. The city looks out across a narrow strait called The Sound (Øresund), towards the Swedish town of Helsingborg. To the west of Zealand passes the wider Great Belt (Storebælt), the main channel into the Baltic Sea.

By August 3rd, John was to the north of The Sound, where the *Dictator* was anchored with the rest of the growing fleet. The British plan required that reinforcements could not arrive to liberate Copenhagen and that the Danish fleet could not leave. British troops under General Wellesley, the future Duke of Wellington, landed near Copenhagen and set up mortar positions. Admiral Keats was given a squadron of ships, the *Dictator* among them, with orders to isolate Zealand from the rest of Denmark and to ensure that no Danish naval ships could escape from the Baltic.

Two weeks after first arriving in The Sound, the *Dictator* took up position off Samsoe, an island to the north of the Great Belt. Concerned at being so close to a hostile shore, Campbell ordered a boat to row guard each night. As a midshipman, John may have spent cool nights in the ship's boat, coat pulled tight around him and eyeglass in his lap, while a party of seamen rowed them slowly round, ready to raise the alarm if he spotted any approaching Danish boats.

The rest of the large British fleet sailed south towards Copenhagen, ready to reinforce the diplomatic message. The first proposal put to the Danish was that they should place their fleet into the safety of British hands until the end of the conflict, coupled with financial inducements and a promise to defend Danish shores against invasion. The Danes declined the offer in terms that the British, perhaps conveniently, chose to see as a declaration of war. A new demand was sent into the city: The price of peace had now changed and required not only the full surrender of the Danish naval fleet but also the delivery of all naval supplies in the royal dockyard and arsenal. The British turned to force to drive the message home and began four days and nights of bombardment from land and sea.

John would have waited with the rest of the *Dictator*'s officers, impatient for news. Samsoe was a good eighty miles from Copenhagen as the crow flies, and reports of how events were unfolding were limited to occasional dispatches and whatever information they could glean from the crews of gun brigs returning for provisions and repairs.

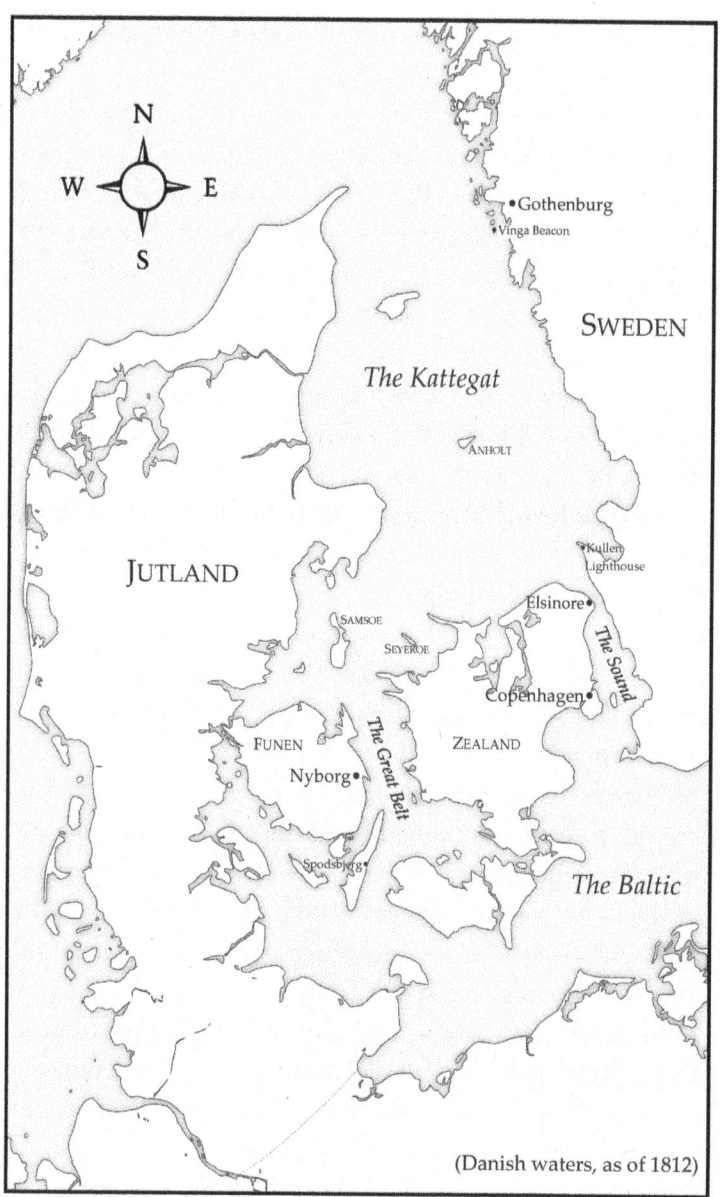

(Danish waters, as of 1812)

Thousands of bombs and rockets rained down on the city each day, among them Congreve incendiary rockets, a new invention and particularly effective on a city built largely of wood. One such rocket hit the city's cathedral, which burned to the ground. On September 7th, faced with over a thousand buildings on fire and a reported two thousand civilians among the dead[14], Copenhagen's leader Ernst Peymann agreed to all British demands and received assurances that the enemy fleet would leave his city within six weeks.[15] In truth, time was of the essence anyway. Winter was approaching and a long delay could see ice appear in the Great Belt and leave the British ships trapped and vulnerable.

When the British fleet left Copenhagen late in October, they took with them twenty-four valuable Danish battleships, each loaded with naval supplies. The mission promised to be a financial as well as a military success for John and every other man involved. The captured fleet and cargo had been taken during a state of war and the prize court in Yarmouth was expected to pay handsomely.

Although the British departed from the Baltic before the winter ice arrived, John experienced the roughest seas and the stormiest weather he had yet encountered in his fifteen months with the Royal Navy as the fleet sailed back through the North Sea. Several Danish prizes, including a large ship of the line, were lost before they reached England.

Later in life, John makes little mention of the Bombardment of Copenhagen in his various accounts. He does reveal, though, that he was put in command of one of the captured prizes. Given the weather they faced on the journey home to England, the young midshipman had good reason to be pleased.

In 1807 I had the honour of being at the Siege of Copenhagen under Admiral Lord Gambier, and was then in command of one of the captured men of war which I brought home safe to Chatham.[16]

A few days after the bombardment, damning reports appeared in the London papers that Britain had launched an unprovoked attack on a friendly nation and had targeted a city of civilians and children. The government was heavily criticised, with accusations that the attack was a stain on the national character. Defence Secretary George Canning justified the need for the attack in parliament with customary eloquence, and wrote tellingly in a private letter, 'We are hated throughout Europe and that hate must be cured by fear'.[17]

Britain's attack on Copenhagen had ensured that the Danish fleet could not be used against it in an invasion but, in doing so, it had brought a new and determined enemy into the conflict. Left without a fleet, Denmark threw its energy and resources into the creation of large numbers of smaller, oared vessels, each mounted with one or two guns. They could move fast over short distances and were not dependent on the wind. These were positioned all along the coast, ideal for attacking British merchant shipping as it passed close to shore while entering or leaving the Baltic. The Gunboat War had begun.

3. Baltic ice

Captain Macnamara was finally successful with his entreaties to the Admiralty for the release of his former midshipmen, and John Monk prepared to reunite with his old captain and mentor on HMS *Edgar* in Plymouth in March 1808. John had served under Donald Campbell for just a year, and it is tempting to overlook the influence Campbell may have had on him, but John's papers suggest the two men had built a good working relationship. In a letter from 1820, he wrote, 'I lost a great friend in Admiral Campbell who died a little time ago in the West Indies'.[1]

John was not joining a happy ship. Macnamara had been having a difficult time on the *Edgar*. His health was increasingly causing him problems.[2] He was suffering badly from rheumatism, a common complaint among sailors, and one made worse by the frequent cold, wet conditions. For much of February and March, Macnamara remained in London, confined to bed with rheumatic fever, where he was also preoccupied with undisclosed personal matters. The Admiralty was sympathetic and granted each of his requests for time off to recover or to sort out his affairs, but there was little support they could offer when his ship was at sea.

All of this had made him irritable and short-tempered when on board, and he was struggling to maintain his authority. His punishments of errant seamen had grown in frequency and severity, and the relationship between officers and men had soured. In theory, a captain was able to issue punishments of up to twelve lashes, and more severe punishments could only be ordered by a court-martial. In practice, though, Macnamara regularly handed out punishments of twenty-four or thirty-six lashes for common offences such as drunkenness or skulking.

To make matters worse, the ship was in the grip of a health crisis. During March alone, twenty-one men had to be discharged to the hospital. A further six men deserted. With a company of more than six hundred men and boys on board, the ship had become an angry, fearful and tense place to live and work.

On March 26th, while Captain Macnamara lay in his sickbed in London, the unhappy situation on HMS *Edgar* finally exploded. The ship was at anchor in Cawsand Bay, on the western side of Plymouth Sound, when the angry crew gathered on deck, shouting and calling for change. The master-at-arms ran below decks to the wardroom and alerted Lieutenant Campbell, one of the few officers on board at the time, who headed to the upper deck and confronted the crew, where the men noisily demanded a 'Fresh Captain and Officers!'.[3]

Lieutenant Campbell ordered the men to return to their duties but without success. As the exchanges grew more heated, he called for the marines, who stood facing the crowd with muskets loaded. Just as Campbell was about to order the marines to open fire, the angry men began to disperse. Five of the most vocal seamen standing nearest to the marines were arrested and put in irons.

The prisoners were sent to HMS *Salvador del Mundo* to await their trial. The court-martial was presided over by Thomas Sotheby, rear-admiral of the blue, who heard the prosecution on Saturday, April 2nd. Lieutenants, marines and midshipmen appeared as witnesses for the prosecution and each recounted a similar version of events. The discontent among the crew ran deep. This was not an isolated group of rabble-rousers. When asked how many men had assembled, witness after witness answered, 'most of the ship's company' or 'at least three hundred'.

The court reconvened on Monday to hear the defence. Each of the accused called a witness to testify that they had been a reluctant participant, who had either acted under duress or had wanted no part of it. Most striking from the transcript is that the underlying causes of the disturbance were neither discussed nor offered in defence. The proceedings were strictly limited to the order of events, whether each man was present and the level of his involvement. Any discussion of Captain Macnamara's culpability for the problems on board would be held behind closed doors at the Admiralty, rather than among a panel of his peers and juniors at a court-martial. For a defendant or witness to suggest he might have a valid grievance would have been to invite a harsher punishment.

All five were found guilty of 'having behaved in a very mutinous and seditious manner',[4] and each was sentenced to at least two hundred lashes. The most severe punishment went to Henry Chesterfield, a twenty-five-year-old Cornishman and the captain of the main-top, considered the ringleader as the only petty officer arrested. He was to receive seven hundred lashes on his bare back, flogging round the fleet, and was to be imprisoned in Marshalsea for two years in solitary confinement.

Flogging round the fleet was a particularly severe punishment given to court-martialled men when the fleet was in harbour.

Chesterfield would have been tied to an upright frame, fixed in place in the *Edgar*'s launch. The boat would then have been rowed alongside the ship, where John would have assembled on deck with the captain, fellow officers and men to witness the punishment on the water below. Chesterfield would have received the first set of fifty lashes, before being rowed to the next ship in the fleet for a further set, and so on until his sentence was complete.

Henry Chesterfield entered Marshalsea Prison in Southwark, South London on September 5th, 1808. Although often remembered today as the debtors' prison in Dickens' *Little Dorrit*, the Admiralty also used part of the prison for seamen convicted of mutiny, sodomy, sedition and desertion. Chesterfield was discharged exactly two years later, although what state he was in after seven hundred lashes and such a long period in solitary confinement is not recorded.[5]

Macnamara's role in creating the hostile mood on board had not escaped the attention of the Lords of the Admiralty, who had reviewed the *Edgar*'s logbook entries for June to December of 1807. In a letter sent after the court-martial, the Lords reprimanded him for the brutality of his regime:

Their Lordships have observed with surprize and concern that, within the space of five months, more than 120 punishments have taken place in the ship under his command and many of them with an unusual degree of severity... ill-calculated to convey a favourable impression of that good order and discipline (for which) His Majesty's Naval Service is generally distinguished.[6]

With the court-martial completed and sentences delivered, Macnamara moved his ship from Plymouth to the Downs. On the first day at sea, he showed his men that his authority had not been damaged by the uprising, in which so many still on board had taken part. Six men faced the lash that day, for various offences including 'mutinous practices', a term that in the current hostile climate could have been applied to any small act of disagreement or defiance.

The Evacuation of Nyborg, 1808

In the year 1808, I was employed in the Baltic and I commanded the boat that took the first Spanish officer off the Danish island which was the means of liberating the army under the Marquis of Romana, when the forts of Nyeborg would not surrender to the Spaniards.

The transfer to the *Edgar* on April 28th came with a promotion. John would now be one of three master's mates, senior petty officers who reported to the ship's sailing master, William Arney. The master reported directly to the captain and the two men would have worked closely together. The captain himself tended to be more expert in warfare and man-management, whereas the master was skilled in sailing and navigation.

As in John's case, a master's mate was often a senior midshipman, still waiting to pass his examination for lieutenant or to receive a commission. He would now directly supervise the quartermasters in steering the ship, take responsibility for fitting her out, make sure she had all the sailing supplies necessary for the voyage, and hoist and lower the anchor, all on the master's instruction, of course. He was also required to examine the ship daily and to notify Arney of any problems.

May 15th was a new low point for Macnamara's harsh regime. Ten men faced the lash, including several who received thirty-six lashes for drunkenness. With the ever-present risk of infection, such punishments could be life changing. The boatswain's mate gave a total of 216 lashes on this one day alone, while John and the rest of the assembled ship's company looked on. The boatswain's mate was often despised by seamen, but his was not always a role to be envied. Better to give the lashes than receive them, but if the supervising officer felt that the mate carrying out the flogging was being too soft, he could be ordered to take the place of the prisoner and to receive the rest of the punishment himself.[7] One of the five men who had been convicted of mutiny in March had been John Rowlands, the boatswain's mate.

At the end of May, with her depleted crew numbers bolstered by thirty men drafted from the sloop HMS *Calypso*, the *Edgar* weighed anchor and John, in his new post, followed the master's orders as they worked their ship out of Yarmouth Roads and into the open sea. Several flat-bottomed boats were in tow, giving an indication of the role that the ship was about to play. John was returning to the Baltic, as part of a squadron under Sir Richard Keats. Having made an enemy of Denmark with the bombardment of Copenhagen, Britain now had to deal with the consequences.

The weather in early June 1808 was hot and sultry as HMS *Edgar* rounded Jutland and entered the Kattegat, the approach to the Baltic. Keats's squadron sailed slowly south, with the coasts of hostile Denmark to the west and friendly Sweden to the east, and then on through the dangerous waters of the

Great Belt, between the Danish islands of Funen and Zealand, a channel barely ten miles wide at some points. Danish gunboats could be seen at intervals along the coast. Any enemy merchant or naval vessel wishing to enter or leave the Baltic had to run the gauntlet, hoping that a favourable wind would allow her to outrun the oared gunboats that emerged from either shore at the prospect of a British prize.

The Royal Navy had to ensure that this crucial trade route remained open. Frigates patrolled the waters and ships of the line kept watch, far enough from shore to be safe from land batteries. Denmark had successfully prevented detailed maps of its coastal waters from being taken abroad, which meant extra work for the *Edgar*'s cooper. As well as barrels for the ship's provisions, he was regularly called on to make buoys to mark out submerged hazards for John and the rest of the master's team, who had to guide their ship through the treacherous shallows.

Every few days, a different convoy of merchant vessels passed through the channel, heading into or out of the Baltic under the protection of a Royal Navy ship. Particularly when the winds were light, the well-drilled oarsmen of the Danish gunboats could catch up with the merchantmen who, without a breeze to fill their sails, were unable to escape. Each time the *Edgar* saw Danish gunboats make for an approaching merchant convoy, the ship's own boats put out to sea as a deterrent. Sometimes the Danes turned back to shore. Other times they did not. During the course of the war, many valuable merchant vessels were captured, as well as several smaller Royal Navy ships. As a reminder of the dangers, a solitary cutter sailed up to the *Edgar* on August 3rd. Inside were a petty officer and six men from HMS *Tigress*, a twelve-gun brig, who reported that their vessel had been captured the previous night by Danish gunboats.

Some boat chases revealed unexpected occupants. On August 1st, 1808, as the *Edgar* patrolled the waters around Funen, John was sent out in command of the ship's cutter in pursuit of a boat and returned, some hours later, with a Spanish officer and several soldiers.[8] It is likely to have fallen to John to break the news to his Spanish prisoners that Napoleon had placed his brother, Joseph Bonaparte, on the Spanish throne and that their home country was in the grip of a popular uprising.

Spain had about twelve thousand troops stationed in Denmark at the time, under the command of Pedro Caro, the Marquis de la Romana, to assist should the British attack again and to prepare for an invasion of Sweden. The French authorities in Denmark had managed to keep news of the uprising in Spain from the Spanish troops in Copenhagen but, when news eventually reached the Marquis, he realised that he and his men had to continue to show allegiance to the French or risk being taken prisoner. The British, naturally, would be only too happy to assist the Marquis, should he and his men desire to return to Spain and defend their homeland. The challenge was how to make contact.[9]

The offer had to be made with the utmost discretion, as the Marquis was being closely monitored by his hosts. In a plot worthy of a spy novel, the British recruited a German-speaking Scottish priest, who made his way to Nyborg posing as a merchant selling coffee and cigars. To speak to the Marquis, the faux-merchant barged into him in the street, apparently by accident, before apologising profusely and offering him some coffee. Switching to Latin, he quietly conveying the British offer of help. After further secret communication, the Marquis and Admiral Keats had settled on a plan.

On the date agreed, August 9th, 1808, the Marquis and his men seized Nyborg's fortress and Keats readied his ships to take possession of the port. He wrote to the Danish governor, threatened to destroy the town and demanded that the Spanish troops be allowed to leave unopposed. Aware, no doubt, of the fate suffered by Copenhagen in 1807 and seeing that he was outnumbered, the governor agreed.

At this point, though, a problem arose. Despite their governor's instruction to capitulate, the captains of the Danish brig-sloop *Fama* and the cutter *Søormen* moored their vessels across the harbour and stubbornly refused to give way. Macnamara saw no option but to remove this obstacle and selected officers for a boat attack, with John among them. As a young and determined officer, John is likely to have embraced this opportunity to prove himself and demonstrate the extent of his abilities and loyalties. He had been stationed eighty miles away during the Battle of Copenhagen but at Nyborg he was to be in the thick of the action.

The officers and men filled the *Edgar*'s boats and rowed into the harbour towards the two blockading vessels, with cutlasses and pistols at the ready. The two Danish vessels fought back against the boarding parties. Each was eventually captured, but only after a fierce fight that left seven Danes and one British officer dead. In the attack on the *Fama*, the larger of the two vessels, John later wrote that he had suffered two broken fingers in his left hand[10].

Over the next few days, the British boats set about ferrying the large number of Spanish soldiers out of Nyborg. Shifting position nearer to Spodsbjerg Battery, Macnamara and his men equipped the many transport vessels that would be needed to carry such a large force. John was given charge of the captured *Fama* and ordered to transport Spanish troops north to the friendly Swedish port of Gothenburg. The transports alone would not be enough to evacuate such an army, and the *Edgar* herself received 217 Spanish soldiers on the 11th and a further sixty-five on the 12th.

As one of three ships of the line employed in the embarkation, the *Edgar* became a centre for diplomatic hospitality. Macnamara and his officers entertained brigadier generals and field officers for several weeks, along with their entourages, wives and families. As captain, it was up to Macnamara to cover the cost of his table. His letters from this time show that this extra hospitality cost Macnamara a small fortune personally, and he spent much of the next year arguing with the Admiralty as he attempted to recover the expense.[11] On August 21st, the *Edgar* and the large convoy of over fifty transports began their journey to the north, up through the Great Belt and into the Kattegat, where the *Edgar* parted company with the convoy near Anholt. The Spanish troops returned to Spain and were brought ashore at Corunna on September 30th, from where they were able to fight for their country in the Peninsular War.

John's active service summaries are rarely very elaborate and sometimes rather messy, but they help to draw out details that would otherwise be lost and also show what John himself felt was important. As he later recalled about the evacuation at Nyborg,

I was slightly wounded in a gun boat under Commander Keats and Captain Macnamara. I was put in command of the Fama, *Danish man of war, to convey a number of the Spanish troops down to Gothenburg.*[12]

With the evacuation complete, the *Edgar* sailed north to Elsinore, where the strait between Denmark and Sweden narrowed to just two miles. Overlooking the channel stood the imposing Kronborg Castle which was operating as a base for Danish gunboats. Convoys of British merchant vessels passed regularly, and each was offered the protection of the *Edgar*'s boats. Admiral Keats sent flags of truce to Elsinore and arranged prisoner exchanges. Prisoners of war were a valuable, tradeable commodity.

By the end of November, winter was approaching and the weather began to turn cold. Squally winds and snow showers were common, and John and his shipmates were greeted on many mornings by thick fog and a heavy frost.

On December 28th, 1808, as conditions worsened, the ship's various records hint at a minor mystery. Macnamara's log states that a seaman, Charles Olliphant, had died the previous day, but then says that bodies (plural) were committed to the deep, with no mention of any other deaths on board. Fortunately, the captain's log is not the only record. The Admiralty demanded that a number of logs were diligently maintained on every one of His Majesty's ships. The captain's log was compiled from the master's log, with additions as he saw fit, although who actually penned either of them is often unclear. There was also a ship's log, updated at regular intervals each day by the officer of the watch. These are often rougher and scruffier, written on coarse grey paper.

Sometimes it is necessary to read between each of these documents to get a fuller picture of an event. The answer to this particular puzzle lies in the day's entry in the ship's log: 'Departed this life, the wife of Wm Nessbit, Surgeon.'[13] The presence of a woman on board may have been considered to be unlucky by some seamen, but the occasional officer's wife might be given dispensation by the captain to travel on the ship. The surgeon and his wife most likely worked together, but she was not on the ship's muster and received no pay. Although arguably correct for Macnamara to exclude her death from his report on those grounds, the consequence is that women like this are almost entirely absent from surviving records.

The winter weather continued to close in alarmingly. As an icy winter storm hit the area, Macnamara ordered the *Edgar* to the north, anchoring nearer to Kullen Lighthouse. It was time for the British ships to leave the freezing Scandinavian waters. As they prepared to do so, though, the storm worsened and strong winds from the east drove already-formed ice into the ships' paths, threatening to block their exit from the Kattegat completely.

Captains' logs routinely makes for very dry reading, in which engagements, boardings and cutting out operations get reduced to brief, perfunctory notes. Just occasionally, though, the entries come alive and describe more fully a moment of drama or danger. On the morning of December 31st, conditions deteriorated further and by mid-morning the *Edgar* was stuck fast in a thick ice sheet. An hour later, through the efforts of the master William Arney, John Monk and the other master's mates, the ship had been freed and sailed slowly onwards, bumping and scraping her way through the field of ice.

The following day, January 1st, 1808, was cloudy with a severe frost. In a report to the Admiralty on his return to Britain, Macnamara described 'an almost impenetrable sheets of ice, which appeared completely to cover the whole of the Kattegat.'[14] Vinga Beacon and Gothenburg lay five miles to the north-northwest. Looking out across the ice, John would have seen the gunboat *Monkey* and a transport close by, and HMS *Superb* (74), *Dictator* (64) and *Orion* (74) some distance away. Macnamara sent a boat out towards the *Superb* but it returned, unable to force its way through the craggy, splintered ice field. The frozen sea had turned each ship into a distant island and each would have to battle her own way through to safety.

The situation seemed hopeless, and the *Edgar* signalled with telegraph flags to Admiral Keats and Captain Samuel Jackson on the *Superb*: 'Are your pilots and master of opinion that you can get out of the Cattlegate (sic)?'[15] The response was a short, but hopefully reassuring, 'Yes'.

John was faced with the same frosty conditions on the morning of January 2nd. The ship had stopped dead, and all hands were employed cutting through the ice. The ship's company worked hard to lighten her load and release her from her frozen grip. Heavy metal objects were heaved overboard at the ice that imprisoned the ship's bow. Shot, capstan bars, crowbars and slabs of iron ballast all went over the side.

There was a jolt in the late morning as the ship began to move, but the release was brief and by the afternoon she was again stuck fast. The men reported back to the captain that the tumbling ice blocks were six feet thick in places. The kedge anchor and an anvil were next to be heaved over the bow in an attempt to break through, and men continued to hack away at the ice with crowbars.

It was hard work but gradually they cleared a path, until finally, by late afternoon, the ship was free. Macnamara ordered the master to make all sail, pleased, no doubt, to put distance between themselves and the ice field.

Their journey across the North Sea could begin, but the challenges continued. The master and his mates struggled to guide the *Edgar* south through strong gales and heavy swell, as her general seaworthiness deteriorated fast. The *Edgar* was a third-rate ship of the line, not an ice breaker with a reinforced frame beneath a thickened hull, and the stresses of the escape from the Kattegat had taken their toll. Every mighty crash and scrape from the ice blocks had twisted and strained the ship's structure, and by January 4th, worrying leaks had begun to appear and the water level in the hold was rising alarmingly. John Monk and the other master's mates continued to check all areas of the ship, and reported each crack, tear or split back to the master. The crew worked ceaselessly to secure the masts with runners and tackles. To lose a mast in the middle of such a storm could be catastrophic and would leave the ship unnavigable and at the mercy of the waves. The captain reported that evening, 'Ship labouring exceedingly, and leaky in every direction'.[16]

The gales and heavy seas continued through Thursday and Friday. The winds split the main topsail, and the sea carried away one of the boats. John's regular reports back to the master on the condition of the ship would have been increasingly concerning. In this bad weather, the ship was taking on nearly four feet of water a day. Seeing that his ship could not reach

Yarmouth in her current condition, Macnamara shortened his journey, first to the Humber and then to the Firth of Forth, as the leaks worsened still further.

As the *Edgar* finally approached the safety of a home port, the wind lessened, the seas grew calmer and the storm slowly began to abate. The master may have pointed out familiar landmarks to John and his other mates as they passed them - Coquets Isle, Bass Rock and Inchkeith, Edinburgh to the south - before they sailed slowly up the estuary, where two pilots came on board and worked the exhausted ship into position.

Not every vessel in the Baltic was so lucky that winter. It would be a full eighteen months after the evacuation from Nyborg before Captain Macnamara appeared before the prize court in February 1810 to claim the *Fama* and *Søormen* as prizes, by which time both of these captured vessels had long since been lost.[17]

The *Fama* had been commissioned by the British under her existing name, and the *Søormen* had become the *Salorman*. On December 22nd, 1808, four months after their capture at Nyborg, when John Monk had proudly ferried Spanish officers in the *Fama* to Gothenborg, both vessels left Karlskrona as part of an escort for the last British convoy of the year to leave the Baltic. The convoy was much further from home than the *Edgar* and as the temperature dropped, so the dangers increased.

On December 23rd, the convoy met the same brutal winter weather front that would hit the *Edgar* in the Kattegat. In the midst of howling winds and blinding snowfall, the master of the *Fama* lost sight of the nearest ship, altered his course and ran aground on the island of Bornholm. The captain, a seaman and a female passenger froze to death during the night. The next day the islanders passed lines to the brig to effect a rescue, but a further four men and a woman died trying to reach the shore. Those who survived were taken prisoner. Other vessels in the convoy also met their end in the same storm, including the *Salorman*. The rest were carried back into the Baltic, unable to get through the ice, where many more were wrecked or captured.[18]

Shore leave, 1809

John Monk spent a foggy, snowy January in 1809 on the Firth of Forth on Scotland's eastern coast, as teams of men patched up his ship and refitted the rigging, and it was March 3rd before she could continue her journey, first to Spithead and then into Portsmouth harbour.

With the *Edgar* delivered into the hands of the dockyard craftsmen, John was granted leave. He took the stagecoach to Chester where he met his parents at the office of a family friend, Solomon Boileau. After many years as cashier of the Dublin Bank, Solomon had retired to Chester, where he would come to an untimely end the following year, drowning one stormy night as he walked home drunk and fell into the River Dee.

Solomon relayed the news of the meeting to Edward Acton Gibbon, his friend and John's brother-in-law, back in Dublin:

I was very agreeably surprised this day week by a kind visit from your brother-in-law young Mr John Monk. He was just arrived from the North Sea, had left his ship (the Edgar*) at Portsmouth,* *and had come over here on a six weeks leave of absence, he looks remarkably well and was in high spirits.*[19]

The view that greeted John, as he and his parents travelled the twelve miles by carriage from Chester to Parkgate, was the familiar rural landscape of gently rolling hills and small hamlets, with houses of distinctive local red sandstone, roofed with Welsh slate. Neston, a mile to the east of Parkgate, was still the largest settlement on the Wirral and held a certain prominence and affluence due to its proximity to Chester, while villages further towards the north-western end of the peninsula, like West Kirby, Wallasey and Birkenhead, remained isolated and relatively inaccessible. Physical geography meant that the Wirral had been largely ignored by the Industrial Revolution during the eighteenth century. To the south, the Dee separated the peninsula from Wales, and to the northeast, the Mersey presented a similar barrier. Sailing services across the Mersey had run in different guises for centuries but were always at the mercy of winds and tides. Fog, which was common on the Mersey, could reduce winds even further.

Much had remained unchanged in John's absence. His father William was still employed by the customs service in Parkgate, where he would remain until his retirement. Benjamin was still working alongside his brother, although a couple of years later he would leave to become the acting customs controller in Chester. Parkgate was still a functioning port, but his father would have reported with likely concern that things were noticeably quieter.

During the first decade of the nineteenth century, maritime trading through Parkgate had dropped off sharply. The large, funnel-shaped Dee estuary remained a place of constantly shifting sediments. It was a natural process, but more recent shifts had been exacerbated by human intervention. Well-intentioned actions could have unintended consequences, and with a limited understanding of fluid mechanics, each change to the channel or either bank represented something of a gamble. An alteration initiated in the 1780s by the River Dee Company had led to a noticeable increase of sediment on the Wirral side.[20] It would be a slow process, but the days were numbered for the port of Parkgate.

William oversaw the collection of duty taxes on the diminishing number of arriving vessels and checked paperwork was in order. He also represented the first line of defence against smuggling, a common problem in the area during the eighteenth century. Tax rates were much lower on the Isle of Man, and there was money to be made by bringing goods over illegally for sale on the mainland. Smuggled goods were often concealed on merchant vessels arriving at Parkgate or were brought ashore in smaller boats on dark and moonless nights.

A portrait from 1819 shows William as a large, friendly looking man, with a smart, striped waistcoat and tufts of fair curly hair protruding from under a top hat.[21] To modern eyes, or to any eyes, in fact, one of the stranger parts of his role as customs officer was undoubtedly the issuance of hair powder certificates. The wearing of wigs had become hugely popular in England during the seventeenth and eighteenth centuries, especially for men of higher social standing, and a wig was almost essential for a formal dress occasion. Most wig wearers were men, as women tended to powder their natural hair or wear extensions. The tax on hair powder had been introduced in 1795 by William Pitt the Younger as one of a series of measures to raise funds for the war with France. Any man wishing to apply powder to his wig was required to pay one guinea or risk a fine. Lists of certified powder users were then published on the door of the parish church and at other locations. Unfortunately for the Tax Office, the charge spelt the end of the Georgian wig-wearing fashion and, as the war ended, young gentlemen in Regency England increasingly chose a more natural hairstyle.

Where William and Benjamin had once overseen a small but busy port, they were now faced with a growing number of tourists and other visitors. A sandstone sea wall and walkway were built in sections from 1810 onwards, and became a stage upon which the ladies and gentlemen of fashionable society could promenade and mingle in their Georgian finery. They did not always have the Parkgate seafront to themselves, however, and the intended atmosphere of sophistication could sometimes be disturbed by groups of youths who liked to hang around on street corners and hurl insults at passers-by.[22]

John's return would have been a chance for his parents to fill him in on the news of his siblings. Elizabeth was in Dublin with her husband Edward, mother of three already and pregnant with a fourth. Charles was recently married, Joseph not. Ann may already have been courting the Chester auctioneer, John Brown. Their youngest, Nessie, was at home, still just a child of ten. There may also have been news of his cousin, Richard, Benjamin's oldest boy, as John was not the only Monk taken far from home by the long war. The two cousins had grown up together in Parkgate, their fathers working side-by-side each day. Richard was the older of two, six years John's senior. When each was old enough for military service, John had chosen the Royal Navy, while his cousin Richard had enlisted with the

Royal Cheshire Militia. William and Benjamin Monk both had reason to scour their newspapers anxiously for fresh reports.

One notable absence at home would have been John's second brother, William. Four years had passed since his untimely death in 1806, aged just 24. The year is recorded in brass in Neston's church but, otherwise, William seems to have disappeared without trace. There is no parish record of his death and he was not buried in the family plot in the Neston church cemetery. The absence suggests either that he died far from home or that his body was never recovered. It is likely that he had embarked on a maritime career, as had three of his brothers, and quite possible that he was working on a Parkgate merchantman, following in the footsteps of his grandfather. A major disaster took place in the Dee estuary in the year of his death, which may provide a clue as to his mysterious demise.

The Parkgate Packet Company had been steadily losing business for several years by this time, but its end was accelerated by the loss of the *King George* in 1806.[23] She had been a new purchase for the company, acquired in a bid to improve its fortunes. The company had chosen poorly, however. The sailing packet had previously been a privateer and had a fine bow and sleek lines designed for speed, not qualities suited to the shallow Dee estuary, where conditions demanded flat-bottomed vessels that could rest at a safe angle when beached at low tide. The sinking of the *King George* on September 14th, 1806, was the worst maritime disaster in Dee history, seemingly the result of no more perilous a circumstance than the tide coming in.

The *King George* sailed from Parkgate at midnight on Sunday at full tide. Most of her passengers were poor Irish seasonal workers, heading home with their earnings after the harvest.

The weather was hazy, drizzly and unremarkable. At half-past one, she ran aground on Salisbury sand bank where she remained for four hours. This was not uncommon, and some of the crew walked on the sand while they waited for the water to return.

The wind changed just as the tide came in, keeping the *King George* on her side as the waves lapped at her hull. Unable to right herself, she filled rapidly with water. Most of the dead were trapped below decks, unable to escape through the hatches. Others died when the mast broke, sending those who had climbed up into the rigging into the dark water below. On the shore, screams were heard through the night air. The death toll varies between reports but there were only six survivors who made it into the *King George*'s boat, and up to 125 lives were lost, although many of the bodies were never recovered.

Whether William was crew on the *King George* is tempting conjecture based on the available circumstantial evidence, but will have to remain just that, in the absence of crew lists and passenger records.

Convoy duty, 1809

As his shore leave came to an end, John Monk said goodbye to his family and was back in Portsmouth before the *Edgar* sailed for the Baltic again on July 1st, 1809. The ship rounded Jutland and continued southwards, down through the Great Belt, west into the Baltic, and on towards the Swedish port of Karlskrona, where much needed provisions could be brought on board.

Allies were increasingly hard to find in this part of the world. Denmark-Norway had been brought into the war by the bombardment of Copenhagen in 1807, and Russia had signed the Treaty of Tilsit with France the same year. Sweden was one of the few remaining friendly nations, although that too changed when the country made peace with Denmark-Norway in December 1809, not long after the *Edgar*'s visit at Karlskrona. A treaty with France followed, leaving Sweden with little choice but to join Napoleon's Continental System. British-flagged ships and merchant vessels were no longer welcome in Swedish ports or coastal waters, although trade would continue unofficially. Later in 1810, Sweden reluctantly declared war on Britain, although it was a bloodless war, with no open hostilities.[24]

The next few months saw the *Edgar* ordered to the Gulf of Finland, John's only venture deep into the eastern Baltic. The master and his mates sailed their ship east towards the coast of Estonia, where the ship's company surveyed the waters around the island of Nargen and put on a noisy show of power in front of the Russian fleet gathered at Tallin. There was then a long wait back in Karlskrona, where Macnamara planned and then cancelled an assault on a cluster of tiny Danish islands, known as Ertholme or the Pea Islands.

By the end of October, Macnamara had new orders. The *Edgar* was to escort a merchant convoy back through the Baltic, first to Gothenburg and then onwards to England. Merchantmen began to gather at Karlskrona in October in anticipation of the convoy's departure. Each merchant master presented his papers to the *Edgar*, and, on November 2nd, guns were secured for sea and the signal was made for a pilot.

Protecting a convoy of merchantmen could be a frustrating task, requiring naval officers to instil order among merchant masters not under their command and who often held them in poor regard. The merchant vessels came in many different shapes and sizes, with different sailing qualities, some fast, some slow. The masters and crew of each vessel might be highly skilled or lacking in ability. Some merchant masters might also consider the convoy process unnecessary and stubbornly decide to make their own way at their own speed. Each day, Macnamara recorded a fluctuating number of vessels in sight. If the merchant vessels were close to the *Edgar*, the threat from Danish gunboats receded. The more spread out the convoy became, the harder it was to offer protection, and the *Edgar* was regularly forced to signal to vessels to make more sail. Each day, though, the slower ones continued to straggle behind. For the sailing master and his mates, it would have been a difficult process, with John and the other mates regularly required to slow the large ship's progress, to allow the accompanying merchant vessels to gain ground.

By November 5th, the *Edgar* and the convoy, with the sloop *Alonzo* (16) and gun-brig *Hearty* (12) in company, had made it as far as Rugen to the south of Copenhagen, where the navigable channel began to narrow and the danger from gunboats increased. The following morning, the *Hearty* went to assist an unknown boat in trouble to the leeward and discovered with delight that the vessel was a French galliot, the *Catharina Christiana*, bound for Riga. Through his years with the Navy, John would see prize money come from a wide variety of sources, and funds from the *Catharina Christiana* included proceeds from the sale of captured vegetable seeds.[25]

By this point, the convoy had grown to a hundred vessels. The demands on the *Edgar* continued to come. One vessel got into trouble, and three men were sent to assist with her navigation. Another of the convoy sprang a leak, so the *Edgar*'s carpenter was sent for an impromptu repair, while another disobeyed Macnamara's signals and received a visit from the ship's cutter. As they passed the south end of Langland, John may have seen that Danish row boats had begun to appear close to shore, keeping abreast of the convoy and looking for vulnerable vessels to target. Anyone who ventured too close in shore was in danger of being picked off.

On the night of November 16th, the captain reported that the sky had lit up with the flash of two guns, and at daylight, the *Edgar*'s cutter and launch returned with a captured Danish sloop, the *Petersdotter*, carrying forty-six oxen and three horses. The livestock could not be taken back to England, so the bullocks were brought on board, and over the next few days the ship's butchers got to work. Unusually, rather than formally presenting the sloop and prisoners to the prize court in England, Macnamara put the Danish seamen back on their now-empty vessel and sent them on their way, minus their valuable bovine cargo.

The convoy was reminded of the risks they faced as they passed the shore battery at Reefness, which opened fire as they drew near. The *Avenger* and the ship's boats went out to encourage those to the rear of the convoy to stay closer to the *Edgar*, but they were unable to save one vessel, abandoned after being hit by a shot. A third prize presented itself to the *Edgar* on November 18th when a small Danish galliot, the *Goede Haab*, was spotted at anchor off Seyeroe Island. As he had with the

Catharina Christiana, Macnamara put his own men on board and added the captured *Goede Haab* to the convoy.

The weather was turning wintery, and John would have felt a chill on his face as the strong, squally wind carried snow and sleet with it. The convoy continued its journey north through the Great Belt, watched again by four gunboats moving along the shore. Several days and nights of stormy seas followed before the convoy reached the safety of Gothenburg on November 25th.

It was time to regroup and take stock. Several vessels in the convoy had reached their destination or could travel no further without repairs. Others were gathered at Gothenburg looking for an escort back to England. During the previous winter, John and his captain had seen first-hand the dangers of leaving their departure from the Baltic too late in the year. The weather worsened further as the *Edgar* put to sea and sailed for home. She was large and heavy enough to weather the storms in the North Sea, but some of the smaller vessels accompanying her laboured in the heavy swell as they journeyed south towards Yarmouth Roads.

The little *Goede Haab* had followed the *Edgar* through the North Sea on her way to the prize court in Great Yarmouth. She was not to prove a very profitable capture for John and his crew mates, however, as the court surveyor declared that many of the old casks of brandy she carried had leaked until almost empty.[26]

4. South to warmer seas

John left HMS *Edgar* on February 25th, 1810, after two years' service as a master's mate, and followed Macnamara once more to his new posting as captain of HMS *Berwick*, together with a handful of other petty officers and two dozen seamen. The *Berwick* was a brand-new, Vengeur-class 74-gun third-rate ship of the line and had been launched less than six months earlier at the Perry shipyard at Blackwall.[1] She was still being fitted out in Sheerness when Macnamara took command. The *Berwick* would be John Monk's home at sea for the next five years.

Months of standing by now followed, while the ship was made ready by warrant officers and different working parties. For Macnamara, it meant a brief respite from the rigours of life at sea, although he did not like the moisture-heavy air of the Medway and North Kent marshlands, which were notorious for malaria. In a letter to the Lords of the Admiralty regarding his health, he complained of 'having been attacked by severe colds and rheumatism during the close of the last campaign in the Baltic', and requested 'a month's leave of absence for the re-establishment of my health, which is much worse since my arrival in this foggy and damp air'.[2] A naval captain with an aversion to fog and damp air was going to find life difficult. Macnamara struggled on through the year, but it was clear that his declining health would force him out of active service before much longer.

John now reported to the *Berwick*'s sailing master, Charles Clayton, but, as the summer of 1810 wore on, they were not doing much sailing. It would only be out at sea that John could truly learn the sailing qualities of this new ship, but he and his fellow master's mates had barely moved from Sheerness for the last six months, except for brief exercises in the Thames and movement up and down the Medway. On Monday, August 6th, Macnamara signalled that his ship was ready to sail, before Clayton and his mates guided the *Berwick* out towards the North Sea for the first time, and onwards to the waters off Westkapelle on the Dutch coast.

As the *Berwick* and other ships gathered off the Dutch coast, the political situation in the Netherlands was changing once again. Napoleon had finally lost patience with his brother Louis and had ordered French troops to the Dutch capital, at which point Louis abdicated and fled. On July 9th, 1810, Napoleon dissolved the Kingdom of Holland and brought the Netherlands directly into the French empire, where he would be free to impose conscription and economic controls.

The months off Westkapelle were uneventful for John and the crew of the *Berwick*, and it may have been a relief to the master and the carpenter when the *Berwick* received orders to return to England, as they could now try to improve the ship's sailing ability. During her first year of service, HMS *Berwick* had not endeared herself to Macnamara's men, who were far from pleased at the state of their new ship. As the master's mate, John's annoyance would have been particularly acute. The ship's rigging and coppered hull were in bad condition, and Macnamara noted with irritation that she was almost unsteerable and sailed 'very heavy'.[3] Frustratingly, these defects had been reported to the Admiralty after an earlier inspection but nothing had been done. The complaints of the *Berwick*'s sailing master and carpenter were being echoed across other Vengeur-class ships. The Admiralty had commissioned forty of these men-of-war from commercial shipyards, but due to corruption and poor construction practices, the forty ships they received were often poorly built. This notoriety gained them the nickname, the 'Forty Thieves'.[4]

The first months of 1811 brought blockade duty. The squadron of British ships outside the port of Cherbourg was stationed off Cape La Hogue and Barfleur, to the east of the peninsula. Each ship made regular visits closer to the port to monitor French activity, noting down the number and size of ships in the harbour and their state of preparedness.

The Royal Navy's blockade of the French fleet had been initiated by the Earl of St Vincent in the Mediterranean. The blockades limited the enemy's opportunity to exercise or gain battle readiness and gave the British early information on any intended naval activity. For the Admiralty, these blockades also served a different purpose. A series of mutinies had occurred in 1797 at Spithead and the Nore, when crews of Royal Navy ships rose up against their awful pay and conditions. News of the first mutinies spread from ship to ship until the Royal Navy was in a state of deep unrest. The mutinies were eventually brought to an end through negotiation and force, but certain lessons were learned. Maintaining the blockade of foreign ports kept unhappy crews occupied, far from shore, and limited the spread of discontent.

It had become an essential part of the war effort, but John, like every young officer, would have quickly discovered that it was cold, dull and repetitive work. It was not the reason any ambitious officer had joined the Navy. There was no glory in it and limited opportunity for prize money. Many days that winter, the ship's deck was thick with snow.

On the morning of March 24th, 1811, the large sail of a frigate was seen moving close to shore, heading west from Le Havre towards Cherbourg along the Normandy coast. Macnamara gave the order to beat to quarters. The ship's drummer beat a rhythm as John and the rest of the crew cleared the ship for action and assumed their stations. It would have been a routine in which John was well drilled, knowing that any non-essential object, if not stowed below, could either hinder movement during battle or become flying debris from enemy fire. Living quarters and decks were cleared, tables and instruments stowed, guns untethered and run out, with gun powder and cannon balls distributed, and the surgeon's table prepared. All to the drum rhythm of Heart of Oak.

The *Berwick* gave chase, but the unidentified frigate found shelter in a small, rocky bay south of Barfleur lighthouse. The frigate would later prove to be *L'Amazone*, Captain Rousseau, which had been attempting again to join the larger French fleet at Cherbourg, hugging the shoreline too closely perhaps, when she had been spotted by the *Berwick*.

The *Berwick* and *L'Amazone* exchanged broadsides, killing one British seaman. As daylight faded, Macnamara decided to stand off for the night. Getting in close to the French frigate would be difficult due to the rocks and shoals, but he had *L'Amazone* cornered and his attack could be resumed in the morning. Aboard *L'Amazone*, Rousseau knew there was no chance of escape. Her rudder had been torn away as she had navigated through the rocks of the bay, leaving her trapped and unable to manoeuvre. During the night, Rousseau evacuated his men and set fire to their stranded vessel. As daylight rose, Macnamara could only watch as the valuable French frigate was engulfed in flames. Looking back towards land before departing, John and others on deck would have seen the wreck of *L'Amazone* being buffeted by the surf on the rocky shore, as casks, the stump of a lower mast and other flotsam floated by.[5]

The French and British navies have different versions of these events. In the British telling, the *Berwick* forced *L'Amazone* into the cove under pressure and her rudder broke off in attempting to escape. In the French account, *L'Amazone* was an easy target, having already run aground due to navigation errors that led to the frigate's pilot being called before the War Council.[6] Macnamara's own write-up suggests the latter may be closer to the truth.

Captain Macnamara left the *Berwick* in October 1811. It was the last time John Monk would serve under him, and the *Berwick* would prove to be the last ship that Macnamara would command. After thirty years at sea with the Royal Navy, the last few years in increasing pain, his health problems may simply have become too much to bear.

Macnamara would be promoted to rear-admiral in June 1814, but never again held an active command.[7] In 1818, he married Henrietta, the widow of Lieutenant-Colonel the Hon. George Carleton. They spent his final years at Clifton, Bristol, where he died in 1826 at the relatively young age of 57.[8] In later years, his old captain's death would prove to be a significant blow for John, who could have benefited from his patronage. Macnamara had given John his first opportunity in the Navy, and they had served together on three ships, in the Channel, the North Sea and the Baltic. When the war was over and peace had finally returned, it would have helped John's cause to have a highly regarded admiral in his corner as he campaigned for promotion.

For now, though, a new challenge and a new captain awaited him.

The Mediterranean fleet, 1811

Macnamara's unexpected departure forced the Admiralty to make alternative arrangements. The next full captain of the *Berwick* was to be Edward Brace, but he was still in the Mediterranean on HMS *St Albans*. Two acting captains bridged the gap between October and November 1811. First came Sir Robert Laurie, captain for a short time while at anchor in The Downs, and then Charles Grant, with whom John Monk sailed south to the Spanish port of Cadiz for a rendezvous with Brace and the *St Albans*. On November 29th, the two captains swapped ships. Captain Grant's trunk and furniture were sent to HMS *St Albans* and, in return, the *Berwick* received those of Captain Brace, after which Captain Grant left the ship and Captain Brace came on board. Brace had entered the Navy in 1781, aged just 11. He had been appointed post-captain by 1800 and had served in the East Indies and the Channel. He was known as a competent captain, but without the hot-tempered edge that had characterised Macnamara.

On December 1st, before unmooring and preparing for sea, John took his place on deck among the assembled ship's company and listened as Captain Brace read out his commission. By mid-afternoon they were underway, passing Cadiz lighthouse and onwards to the Balearic Islands and their destination, Port Mahón, the British base on the south-east of the island of Minorca. For the next four years, through to Napoleon's final surrender and the coming of peace to Europe, Captain Brace, John Monk and the rest of the six-hundred-strong company of the *Berwick* were to be part of Sir Edward Pellew's Mediterranean fleet.

Mahón was a lively and bustling town, with attractive, red-roofed buildings rising up the Minorcan hillside, renowned for its busy social life and the beauty and hairstyles of its women, but the typical Royal Navy seaman saw none of this. While in port, most of the ship's company were confined on board. The marines were often sent onshore to exercise, and Brace may have granted shore leave to John and his fellow officers, but this was a freedom rarely given to seamen, many of whom had been pressed into service against their will.

Among a company of six-hundred men, it was often the same few seamen who faced the lash. Patrick Dowling, an ordinary seaman, received twelve lashes in January for insolence, another thirty in February for skulking and on October 12th he faced a court-martial on HMS *Hibernian* for attempting to commit 'the unnatural crime of buggery on Joseph Wilson, a landsman belonging to the same ship'.[9] Rear-admiral Israel Pellew, brother of the more illustrious Edward, and an assembled panel of nine captains listened to the evidence and sentenced Dowling to three hundred lashes, flogged around the fleet. Dowling's troubles were not finished yet, though, as early in December he received a further twenty-four lashes for attempting to desert.

As of 1812, Britain and its allies were grouped into the Sixth Coalition. Napoleon's fortunes were beginning to turn, as he encountered a series of defeats, most notably the failed invasion of Russia and the loss of Spain to the Duke of Wellington in the Peninsular War. The French empire was contracting, and its enemies were growing in number and confidence.

In early May, the men of the *Berwick* took their ship north from Mahón and took up position with the British fleet outside Toulon, where they would remain through to August. Blockading a port was dull work, as John had learned in the Channel. Every couple of weeks the *Berwick* would take her turn to reconnoitre the enemy's ships in the port. On most days, though, the sailing master James Reeves and his mates executed careful manoeuvres to keep station, maintaining the correct position among the blockading ships.

The French fleet in the Mediterranean rarely ventured far from port. Pellew kept a small squadron of seventy-four-gun ships like the *Berwick* positioned close inshore to maintain the blockade, while the larger part of the British fleet was stationed further from port. Aware of this, French ships would put to sea, conduct their exercises and head back to safety.

Daily routine on board continued, with all the activity needed to keep the ship ready for action and functioning smoothly. There was always a great deal of cleaning on a man-of-war, some necessary but much of it designed simply to keep men occupied. The men washed the decks and scrubbed their hammocks. Supply vessels arrived with barrels of water and beer, and took away empty casks. Bullocks and sheep were delivered to the ship and then butchered within a couple of days.

The heat of the Mediterranean summer was upon them. John would have had a light breeze to refresh him when on deck, but below decks, even with gun ports and hatches opened, he would have found the ship hot and airless. Despite the sunshine and energy-sapping heat, his ship remained at war and had to be ready to intercept enemy merchant vessels at short notice, or to engage the enemy fleet should it emerge from port. The gun crews and marines exercised regularly, and the gunner continued to turn the barrels in the magazine to stop the gunpowder from settling.

A week's return to Mahón in September 1812 gave John, as he turned 21, the opportunity to sit his examination for lieutenant. One benefit of the uneventful months blockading Toulon was that it would have allowed him time to study.

The examination had been introduced in 1677 by Samuel Pepys in his role with the Naval Board. Every candidate for lieutenant faced a similar process. John would have been required to produce journals and logs documenting his service, and then appear before a board of three experienced naval captains who would verbally set him problems, such as describing a difficult situation then asking, 'What orders do you give to your men?'. John may have taken confidence from his years as a master's mate, but this was a proper test of his ability. The tests ensured that the Navy's commissioned officers met a certain standard for seamanship and other necessary skills, but it did not guarantee successful candidates an opportunity to advance. This was Georgian England after all, and the power of influence and family connections still held sway. John duly passed the examination, but he would remain as a master's mate for a further two years before Captain Brace gave him his first commission as lieutenant in 1814.

Prize captures and cutting out operations, 1813

I had the honour of commanding a party of seamen when we landed and took the forts and harbour of Cavalarie, and a large convoy of 22 merchant vessels under the protection of the French National xebec Fortune, *of 10 long 8 pounders and 4 swivels, commanded by Lt Felix Lecamus.*[10]

While anchored at Mahón through the winter of 1812, John and the men of the *Berwick* would have watched from the deck and through the gun ports as ships returned with their captured vessels, each one a potential financial windfall for the captain and company. Fortunes were about to change for the Berwickians, however, and the next few months would prove to be among the most eventful and most profitable that John would see in the Mediterranean.

With the arrival of spring in 1813, the *Berwick* put to sea and joined forces with the frigate HMS *Euryalus* (36), Captain Charles Napier. By early May, the two ships were stood offshore, watching a convoy of twenty French merchant vessels gathered nervously beneath the Martello tower that guarded Cavalarie Bay, east of Toulon.[11] The two captains agreed to share any prize money and discussed their next move.

The smaller *Euryalus* was to approach the bay, from where a ground assault could be launched from the boats of the *Berwick* under the orders of Lieutenant Henry Johnston Sweedland, assisted by master's mate John Monk and a midshipman, Maurice Crawford. For several days, while the surf was too great for boats to land, the men waited, likely with a sense of impatience and anticipation. On Sunday, May 16th, conditions were right, and Sweedland, Monk and Crawford led the boats through the waves and towards the shore. Reaching land, they successfully captured the tower, and turned its guns on the retreating defenders.

The largest vessel in the bay at Cavalarie was *La Fortune*, a French xebec with a crew of ninety-five men, commanded by the impressively named Lieutenant Félix Marie Louis Anne Joseph Julien Lecamus. Facing the combined fire now from *Euryalus*, the *Berwick*'s boats and the guns of the captured tower, Lecamus abandoned ship, but not before firing a shot through her hull and laying a trail of powder to the magazine. Whether the British boat crews were aware of this when they boarded her is not recorded, but they were in time to stop the magazine igniting. *La Fortune*'s guns were hoisted onto the *Berwick* to lighten her load and, with their prize now sitting higher in the water, the ship's carpenter was able to mend her damaged hull.

Monk, Sweedland, Crawford and the men in the *Berwick*'s boats helped to capture over twenty vessels that day. The largest fourteen were brought out as prizes, with valuable cargos of oil, corn and lemons. The raid had not been without loss of life, though. In the chaos of battle, a seaman from the *Euryalus* was killed, and Thomas Johns, a marine from the *Berwick*, was a victim of what is now known as friendly fire, having been 'unfortunately shot by accident onshore'.[12]

For John Monk, the day had been a personal success. Young

officers longed for opportunities to distinguish themselves as Monk, Sweedland and Crawford had at Cavalarie Bay. The three young officers were all named by Brace in his letter to the Admiralty, which in turn was published in *The London Gazette* on Tuesday, July 6th, 1813.[13] The line between glory and death was a fine one, though. Six months later, Sweedland would be dead, killed in another boat action alongside John.

John seems to have taken particular pride in these excursions onto land, which held a special place for him as an opportunity to draw favourable comparisons between the conduct of his fellow seamen and their army rivals. Writing many years later in support of another claim for promotion, John gave his verdict:

I can assure you that the sailors astonished both officers and men of the army in their bravery in the taking of Leghorn, Lazzara, Genoa, Savona and a number of places too many to mention.[14]

In many situations, particularly a boat action like at Cavalarie Bay, a seaman's most valuable weapon would have been his cutlass. These were short swords, sharpened by the ship's armourer and issued to seamen ahead of battle. They were portable, reliable and deadly in close combat, amid the noise, smoke and chaos of a boarding party. Pistols were also suitable at close quarters, but they were single-shot, muzzle-loading, smoothbore weapons and had significant drawbacks. They were difficult to aim with any confidence and took precious time to reload after firing, which hours of practice could reduce but not eliminate.

Two of John's small daggers and four of his pistols are still in the collection of his family. Of the pistols, two have heavy, rounded handles which could double as a cosh if needed. The daggers or dirks are ceremonial, associated with his dress uniform. The blades are ornate, the handles ivory, and one is in its leather-lined gold-plated sheath, engraved with *John Monk, Esq. Royal Navy*. The absence of a rank suggests they date from these years as a midshipman or master's mate.

Capturing multiple small vessels at Cavalarie presented a new problem. To be declared as prizes, they first needed to be sailed from the French coast to the prize court in Mahón on Minorca, during a period of strong winds and rough seas. The smallest vessels were towed, and others sailed alongside the *Berwick*. Brace sent *La Fortune* out to shepherd the smaller boats. The weather improved as the journey continued but progress was still slow. The vessels were in varying states of repair and some were small boats designed for coastal journeys, not properly seaworthy. It took the *Berwick* and her little flotilla a full eight days to reach Mahón on May 24th, with one seaman lost overboard from one of the smaller prizes.

After a largely uneventful summer on blockade duty, John's ship was permitted to roam quite freely during the autumn of 1813, and a flurry of smaller prizes came his way. The first was *St Napoleon*, a flat-bottomed coastal trading vessel, captured underway from Naples to Marseilles. Brace entrusted John with the delivery of the prize to Mahón, along with her French master and the cargo of pumice stone, liquorice paste and orange peel. Time was of the essence as her hull was leaky, and John's crew of eight were forced to man the pumps continually. John appeared before the prize court on September 16th, where he petitioned for an immediate sale at auction, as the cargo was at risk.[15]

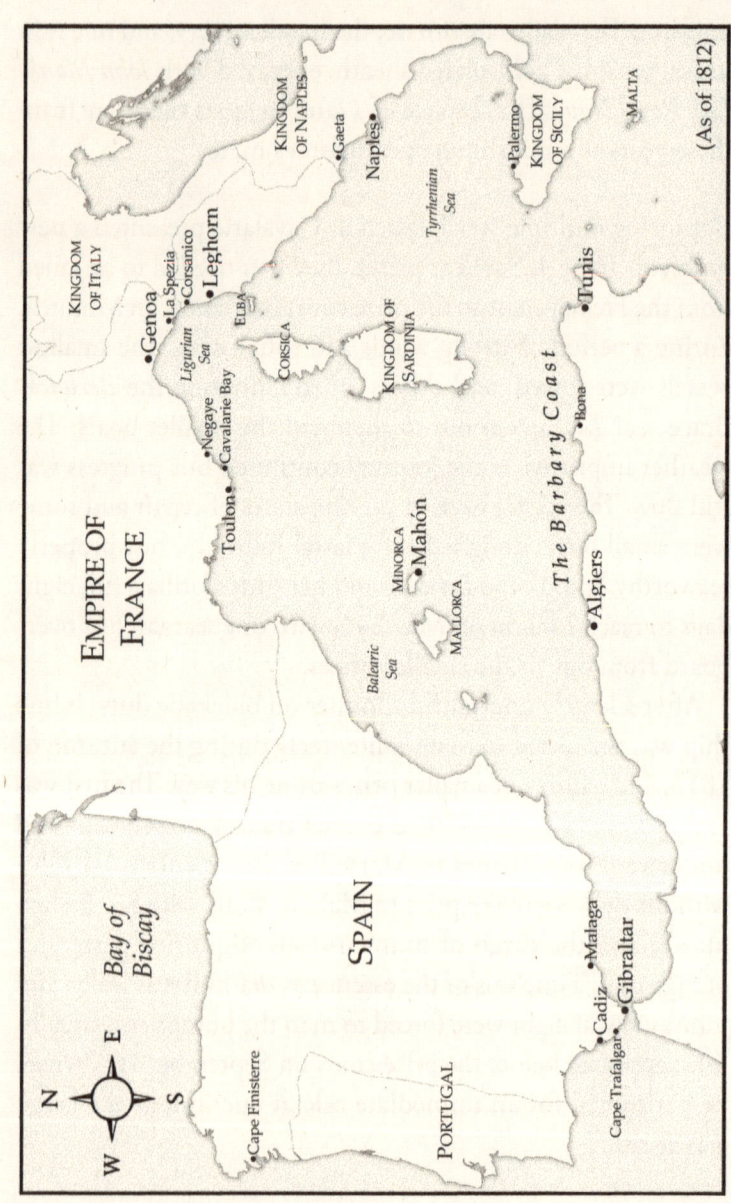

(As of 1812)

EMPIRE OF FRANCE

SPAIN

PORTUGAL

Bay of Biscay

KINGDOM OF ITALY

KINGDOM OF NAPLES

KINGDOM OF SICILY

MALTA

KINGDOM OF SARDINIA

CORSICA

ELBA

The Barbary Coast

Ligurian Sea

Tyrrhenian Sea

Balearic Sea

MINORCA

MALLORCA

Genoa

La Spezia

Corsanico

Leghorn

Gaeta

Naples

Palermo

Tunis

Bona

Algiers

Toulon

Negaye

Cavalaire Bay

Mahón

Malaga

Gibraltar

Cadiz

Cape Trafalgar

Cape Finisterre

N
E
S
W

Two small coasting vessels were captured near Cape Cavalarie on November 13th, followed just three days later by a French poleacre brig, the *St Anne of Genoa*. On both occasions, the prizes were unmanned at the point of capture, the crews having wisely fled onshore to safety on the approach of the British boats. When presented at the prize court, the vessels and their cargo raised a healthy $14,000 at auction. The cargo of eighty thousand oranges and lemons was more valuable than the boats themselves.[16]

Boarding attacks, known as cutting out operations, had become a popular tactic during the eighteenth century, but they were dangerous and often involved hand-to-hand combat with pistols and cutlasses. The element of surprise could be the difference between success and failure, so, where possible, attacks were conducted at night. Officers and selected seamen rowed the ship's boats in near silence through the darkness, towards an anchored vessel, hoping to evade any lookouts and to be alongside before they were detected. After that, it was a step into the unknown for the boarding party. Everything which followed would depend on whether they were met with a quick surrender by the prize's commander or a bloody determination to repel the enemy boarders.

Not all cutting out operations went to plan, and the pursuit of prizes could prove deadly. On the night of December 10th, 1813, the seamen and marines of the *Berwick* launched a boat attack against a convoy of merchant vessels moored in the port of Negaye (modern-day Port Agay) to the west of Cannes. The spirits of John Monk and his fellow officers may have been buoyed by their recent successes, but the assault at Negaye did not proceed so smoothly, due in part to flaws in its planning.

The port had been reconnoitred under cover of darkness the previous night, and the *Berwick*'s officers knew they would have to silence the Martello tower that guarded the bay if they were to be successful. After nightfall, John and Lieutenant Francis Brace, the captain's nephew, with a party of seamen and marines, quietly came ashore nearby and stormed the tower as planned, capturing it at midnight without loss of life. They signalled for the ship's boats, and with Brace in control of the fort, John and a party of seamen headed down to the boats below. As the *Berwick*'s boats entered the port, however, they found themselves facing two heavily armed French navy schooners lying at anchor alongside the smaller merchant vessels, which the previous night's foray had somehow failed to identify.[17] The schooners opened fire on the *Berwick*'s boats as they drew near.

Isolated in the bay, under heavy fire and with their fellow seamen in control of the fort, the *Berwick*'s boats had little choice but to continue. Lieutenant Sweedland, so recently the hero at Cavalarie, now in command of the first boat, went to board the nearest schooner, *L'Estafette*. The French crew fought back hard and killed many of the boarders, with Sweedland among them. She was eventually sunk, but only after Lieutenant Brace in the captured fort turned its guns on her.

Finding himself to be the most senior officer in the bay, John took charge of the launch and the second barge and went to board the second schooner, *L'Air*, commanded by Joseph Toussaint Bernard, son of an eminent French general. A bloody and violent struggle ensued with *L'Air*'s crew of seventy-four. As John reported,

Several men were killed and wounded in the second barge under my command, amongst whom was Mr JH Whitshed, son of Admiral Sir James Hawkins Whitshed, Baronet GCB, who fell mortally wounded at my side.[18]

His recollections of other actions often read with the same brevity and dryness as his captain's log entries, but John's notes on Negaye are unusually vivid. The same is true for his entry in *A Naval Biographical Dictionary*,[19] prepared by William O'Byrne in 1849, in which the account of the night's events reads like an adventure story, right down to 'Mr. Monk and his party, with three cheers, dashed alongside the first schooner, and, after a bloody struggle, carried her'.

The British boat crews eventually prevailed and captured *L'Air*, along with her cargo of gunpowder and muskets. They were not yet out of danger, though. John found that his men were facing sudden, unexpected fire from the captured fort. In the chaos and confusion of battle, Lieutenant Brace had not realised that the French vessel was now in the British boat crew's possession. John needed to leave the harbour quickly. He ordered the prize's anchor cable to be cut with an axe, in an emergency manoeuvre that gives us the modern phrase 'to cut and run'. As *L'Air* sailed slowly towards safety, John and his men passed the first British boat, in which they found the bodies of Sweedland and the rest of his party, all dead.

Many years later, when preparing his application for the Naval General Service Medal, John would contact Francis Brace for a testimonial, feeling that the captain's nephew owed him a favour, having fired on him accidentally at Negaye. John would also recall the 'severe loss on our side of the first lieutenant, one midshipman and twenty men killed and wounded'.[20] The losses had indeed been severe, and John expressed his doubts as to whether news of the boat action at Negaye was ever properly reported. Certainly, it was not recognised with a clasp when the Naval General Service Medal was issued in 1849:

I don't believe the unfortunate affairs of Negaye was ever reported to the Admiralty. Lord Exmouth was so much put out of the way, having so many brave fellows killed.[21]

Further prizes followed in quick succession before John and his shipmates returned to Mahón at the end of December 1813. *La Resurrection* was captured off St Tropez, laden with wheat, and *L'Antoine Camille* was boarded while carrying salt to Leghorn. A larger prize presented itself on December 22nd, when the *Berwick* and ships in company chanced upon schooner *La Fleche*, which had been carrying troops from Toulon to Corsica.[22]

On their arrival back in Mahón, in recognition of John's role in the capture of the schooner *L'Air* at Negaye, Brace ordered him to appear at the prize court on HMS *Berwick*'s behalf. John stood before the British Consul as his ship's representative, flanked by a quartermaster and a seaman and presented the particulars.

The auction sales of the vessels and cargoes captured during the autumn netted nearly $50,000. This would, of course, be shared with any other ships involved, and then divided between captain and crew in line with the rules. It is easy to see how a captain could amass a tidy fortune from such earnings, but even for a master's mate like John, the autumn's prize money would have increased his annual income several times over.

A first commission, 1814

I saw much engagement in boats… assisting the British army under Lord William Bentinck taking the Coast of Italy. I was appointed flag officer on shore at the taking of several towns… and commanded a party of seamen onshore at the Siege of Genoa.[23]

1814 would prove to be the year when the stars would finally align and bring John his first commission, as one of five lieutenants on the *Berwick*, through a combination of his own good conduct and the misfortune of others. The year would also mark the start of John's deep affection for Italy.

The *Berwick* carried John eastwards as spring arrived. Brace's orders were to join up with Sir Josias Rowley's squadron off the Italian coast and to support the slow march north of Lord William Bentinck's British-led land forces.[24] The Republic of Genoa had first been occupied by the French revolutionary army in 1797, when Napoleon had removed the government of old elites and had established the Ligurian Republic. This had been a popular move initially but eight years later the region had been fully annexed into France. Tensions in the city were running high and revolt was in the air.

An initial force of seven thousand British troops had landed at Leghorn on March 9th, 1814, and had marched and ridden north through Pisa, and a second force landed in the Gulf of Spezia after a short siege. As the troops continued their advance on the city of Genoa, the *Berwick* provided offshore support in whichever way it was needed, whether it was hospital facilities for wounded soldiers, receiving French prisoners of war, or seeking to neutralise whichever fort or gun position stood in the troops' way. Boats and marines were landed at strategic points to attack enemy positions from the sea, intending to weaken French resistance and clear the path for the British forces as they approached from the south. One of the *Berwick*'s lieutenants, George Lyon, was wounded, and two seamen were killed in an attack on French mortar positions near the Pass of Rona on April 9th and 10th. [25] The boat crews were busy every day, while the ship's carpenter made scaling ladders and the seamen exercised with small arms and broad swords, in preparation for the expected conflict ahead.

The troops reached Genoa on April 17th, where they found the British ships gathered outside the port, readying themselves for an assault on the city. The following morning, on Captain Brace's command, gun and mortar vessels and the ships' boats, armed with cannonades, moved in and opened fire on the city's gun positions, while Captain Thompson in the *Aboukir* conducted a false attack to the west of the town to draw off as many troops as possible. The strategy was successful and the French defenders retreated inside the city walls.

A full-scale assault or bombardment looked imminent. Seamen and marines were positioned in transport boats, and the *Berwick*'s launch was sent inshore with scaling ladders, ready to storm one of the hill forts. Further bloodshed was averted, however, when the garrison commander agreed to discuss terms, and by April 21st the British had occupied the city. John could now look forward to a spell on land. Captain Brace was appointed naval commissioner and, with the end of French rule, it would take time for Bentinck to establish a temporary local government.

Beyond the Italian peninsula, a hard-won peace was spreading through Europe during these early months of 1814. Coalition forces moved through France and closed in on Paris. Bonaparte put up a brave defence but was overwhelmed, and coalition troops captured the city at the end of March. Bonaparte abdicated on April 6th and, under the terms of the Treaty of Fontainebleau, was exiled to the Mediterranean island of Elba, off the Italian coast. The allies made peace with Louis XVIII's provisional government, headed by Charles Maurice de Talleyrand, and signed the first Treaty of Paris on May 30th, 1814, which reduced France to its 1792 borders.[26]

The *Berwick* lay at anchor in Genoa harbour throughout the Italian summer. Many of John Monk's days were spent on shore, where large groups of marines and seamen cleared the city's arsenal of its valuable contents. Other parties took control of the captured French ships in the city's port. Among these, the British gained possession of four brig corvettes and a brand-new seventy-four-gun ship, which they found in the shipyard, almost ready for launching. The British renamed her from the *Brilliant* to HMS *Genoa*, and the *Berwick*'s crew spent much of July making the *Genoa* ready to sail back to England.

During this first visit to the city in 1814, a chance encounter led to a deep and lasting friendship between John and an Italian family. As he recounted to his nephews later in life, he was walking through the city when he chanced upon a young Italian girl being harassed by a group of 'ruffians'. John intervened and was able to rescue her, losing only her basket of vegetables.[27] The girl was Teresa Massone, the youngest daughter of Marcello Massone, a wealthy and highly regarded local lawyer and probably one of the newly appointed interim governors of the city. Teresa was one of six siblings, with an older sister Norina, and four younger brothers, Marco, Pietro, Carlo, and Giuseppe. A series of letters to John from the Massone family records the developing friendship.

The Massones had a large house in Carignano, on a hill overlooking Genoa harbour, where the father Marcello entertained Captain Brace and the officers of the *Berwick* during the summer, perhaps as a gesture of thanks after John's intervention. A deep mutual affection developed between the Massones and John, who quickly became a regular visitor to the family home. These would have been moments of idyllic respite from the conflict. He joined the family on feast days and for dances, walked with them in the Recco countryside and gave Teresa and her brothers lessons in English.

Two years had passed since John had sat his lieutenant's examination in Mahón in 1812 and, in April 1814, while his ship lay at anchor in Genoa, Captain Brace finally gave him the promotion he sought. His commission was confirmed by the Admiralty in June that year. Brace's demonstration of confidence in John seems deserved. John had shown himself to be an enthusiastic and dependable midshipman and master's mate, who routinely volunteered for cutting out operations, such as those at Negaye and Cavalarie Bay, and he had been entrusted with the command of various prizes.

As is often the case, though, there was also a degree of luck involved. John's eventual promotion was likely hastened by the death or injury to three existing lieutenants in the previous months. Lieutenant Henry Johnston Sweedland had been killed in December during the raid on Negaye, and Lieutenant Edward Witherston had been taken ill at Arans and sent to the hospital, where he later died, aged 22. More recently, Lieutenant George Lyon had been wounded during the attack on enemy posts near the Pass of Rona. Furthermore, John's promotion also allowed Lieutenant Francis Brace to return to England at the end of April.

Although John was the most junior of the *Berwick*'s five lieutenants, it was a significant step up. It brought him a salary of just over £100 per year, a larger share of prize money and greater prestige. The most senior among the lieutenants, the First, ran the ship for the captain day to day and, between the five of them, they were in charge of deck watches and ensured the men carried out their duties. In action, John could expect to lead boarding parties in the ship's boats, or to command a gun deck, as he would later do at Algiers.

After the Peace of 1814, we were left at Genoa to build the Genoa *74 and get all the stores & guns off and sent to England, where we arrived the latter end of the year.*[28]

With the work to clear the city's arsenal and to ready the new ship *Genoa* duly completed, the *Berwick* departed Genoa on August 1st, 1814. John was heading back to England for the first time since leaving three years earlier, in 1811.

For the Massone family back in Genoa, John's departure had been a sad occasion, and the family continued to worry about his welfare. Teresa wrote to him after he left:

We set out for the country the same day you sailed, we were extremely moved when we saw the ship sailing, and still more when the white flag gave us the sign of your Farewell. We never ceased all the day to look at you, and if in the afternoon the Ship had not been so far, we were decided to come on board to see you once more, and give you the last Adieu. But it should not have been the last. We keep your letters, and we read them very often: we know your constant promises, and we shall not die without seeing you again.[29]

John had certainly made an impression on the family. His portrait hung in the Massone house, and Teresa wrote to him that she took comfort from a canary John had left behind, which sang to her with a sweet voice. Each new letter she received from John was added to an ornate wooden box, which he had given her as a gift early in their friendship.

Teresa continued to write to John regularly during the final months of 1814, sending playful letters written with the infatuation of a teenage girl for a dashing young officer, although we don't, unfortunately, have his replies. In her letters, she relayed some of the family's news but spoke mostly of her deep longing to see John again. John was several years older than the teenage Teresa, and her continued passion was seemingly not reciprocated to the same degree. After 1815, she added only brief, polite notes to her father's letters. While Teresa's affections for John cooled, her father's fondness for him remained. Teresa's father Marcello started to treat John as one of his own children. John called Marcello 'Papa', and Marcello referred to his wife Tomasina in letters as John's 'Genoiza Mama'.[30]

How far the romantic feelings had developed between John and Teresa during the summer of 1814 is hard to assess. Teresa was 16 to John's 23, and her early letters show her in a dizzy whirlwind of longing:

I want nothing but your Eternal Love and Friendship. I am

sure that you never forget me, for in an hour that you have been on shore at Leghorn, you thought immediately to me. You say that the few days you have been away looked to you like a month, and they seemed to me a year. I cannot determine myself to destroy your precious letters for they are too dear to me... Adieu my darling, nothing can give me more pleasure than writing to the one I love as much as I love myself. Adieu God bless you.[31]

John may indeed have displayed the conduct befitting of an officer of His Majesty's Navy. That said, there are indications in his later life that he was flirtatious, even roguish, by nature. The truth of their relationship remains tantalisingly opaque.

The Siege of Gaeta, 1815

On Bonaparte's escape from Elba, we were ordered out at a day's notice.[32]

With Napoleon Bonaparte exiled to the island of Elba in April 1814, and Europe ready to enter a time of peace, the complicated process of demobilisation could begin. The Royal Navy had grown many times larger since 1793 and had an urgent need to reduce the size and cost of its fleet. Several officers were discharged from HMS *Berwick* on September 9th, and within the next month, almost half the ship's company were also discharged or put on leave.

By early 1815, though, it became clear that the previous year's optimism may have been premature, and John's expectations for the year ahead took an unexpected turn with some news from the Mediterranean.

Napoleon Bonaparte's exile had ended suddenly on February 26th, 1815, when he had landed on French soil close to Cannes. He had travelled north to Paris, raising support as he went and, by March 20th, Louis XVIII had been forced from the throne and Bonaparte set up a government, marking the start of the period known as the 'Hundred Days'. In response, Britain, Russia, Prussia, Sweden, Switzerland, Austria and the Netherlands acted quickly and formed the Seventh Coalition. While they gathered their armies in Belgium, Bonaparte raised a new Grand Army of his own and headed north, planning to attack before his enemies had organised themselves.

War was also breaking out again in southern Italy. The Kingdom of Naples had been governed since 1808 by Joachim Murat, husband of Napoleon's sister Caroline. Murat had initially appeared a good choice as he had ruled in keeping with his brother-in-law's modernising ethos, introduced the Napoleonic Code and broke up the large estates of wealthy landowners. By 1813, however, seeing that Napoleon's fortunes were waning, Murat signed a treaty with Austria, a shrewd move that allowed him to remain as King of Naples in 1814. These newly declared loyalties proved short lived, however. As Napoleon returned to Paris from exile, Murat switched allegiances once more and declared war on Austria.[33]

Captain Brace, John and the rest of the hastily reassembled ship's company of the *Berwick* were ordered back to the Mediterranean without delay. En route, they were reminded that Napoleon's forces were not the only danger sailors faced in these waters. The *Berwick* anchored briefly off the Moroccan coast and sent a boat ashore to gather sand, commonly used to clean the ship's decks. The boat hurried back, missing one petty officer and four seamen. As John and every man on the *Berwick* would have been aware, North African pirates routinely captured European sailors and sold them into slavery in Algiers and other cities along the Barbary Coast. On this occasion, though, the problem was quickly resolved and the five men were returned safely by the Moorish guard under a flag of truce later the same day.

The British were on high alert when the *Berwick* arrived back in Genoa. The Neapolitan War with Austria had ended with the Battle of Tolentino on May 3rd, and the defeated Murat had fled to Corsica, disguised as a Danish sailor.[34] In the days that followed the battle, the Admiralty received intelligence that a French frigate had entered the port of Gaeta, fifty miles to the north of Naples, raising fears that members of the Bonaparte family were also about to be smuggled away. The *Berwick* and the larger, eighty-gun HMS *Malta* were immediately ordered out and arrived at the Bay of Gaeta on May 19th. Austrian ground forces arrived a few days later and laid siege inland.

Gaeta was governed by Alessandro Begani, a seasoned Italian general who had returned to Italy from exile alongside the army of Joseph Bonaparte in 1806. His town was small but possessed a fortress with excellent fortifications, which Begani had recently strengthened. With Murat's regime at an end, the Anglo-Austrian commanders demanded Begani's immediate surrender, but found themselves faced with a situation they had not expected. Despite Murat's defeat, Begani declared he would defend his town. So began the siege and gruelling two-month bombardment for which John Monk would, many years later, receive the first bar on his Naval General Service Medal.

The Austrian troops began to pound the fortress from their

gun positions, while HMS *Malta* and *Berwick*, at anchor outside of the bay, coordinated the attack from the seaward side. The carpenter and armourer fitted out the ships' boats with guns and mortars, and each night, John Monk and his fellow lieutenants led their boats in through the shallow waters to mount their own attacks on Gaeta's coastal batteries.

It would have been a gruelling routine, snatching sleep during the day ahead of the nightly bombardment. Many of the attacks were intentionally launched after nightfall, when John and the others in the boats would have been less visible to the town's defenders.

The gunboats returned regularly to the large ships of the line for crew rotations or to replenish supplies of provisions and ammunition. The ship's armourer was also busy, keeping the gunboats seaworthy. The force of the recoil from the guns put a strain on the boats, and several times the wooden carriages holding the guns in place worked loose.

The gunboats and batteries continued to exchange heavy fire through June, and the weather turned stormy in July, with thunder, lightning and rain. Flags of truce were flown regularly as boats headed to and from the town, but the siege continued. On July 6th, the British fleet received some good news. Napoleon's army had been defeated on June 18th at Waterloo by the armies of the Seventh Coalition under Wellington, a personal victory for John's cousin, Richard, as he would later discover. News of the battle, and of Louis XVIII's restoration, did nothing to dampen Begani's resolve, however. The Napoleonic Wars were over, Murat had been driven from the Kingdom of Naples, and the Bourbon monarchy had been restored. But on the east coast of Italy, the little town of Gaeta remained as a final corner of Europe under Napoleonic rule. Fahie expressed his exasperation at Begani in his letters to the Admiralty:

The destruction of Buonaparte's hopes and the restoration of His Majesty Louis the 18th have been communicated to the Governor of Gaeta, but he persists in his defence of the place. This conduct can only be the effect of despair, for it cannot be accounted for on any reasonable principle.[35]

The Austrians and British intensified their attack and launched a simultaneous three-day bombardment on July 16th from land and sea, until the guns from the sea-face of the fortress had finally been silenced. The siege continued, but after two exhausting months of near-daily exchanges of heavy fire, the boat crews' efforts were complete. On July 23rd, Captain Fahie sent the *Berwick* to join the rest of the fleet in Genoa. Remarkably, while several hundred Austrian soldiers and a similar number of Begani's men died during the siege, at the point of their departure, HMS *Berwick* had only one casualty, a landsman who had to have his left arm amputated after a gunshot wound.

The *Berwick* followed the familiar line of the Italian coast as she headed northward, with gunboats in tow, leaving the Tyrrhenian Sea around Naples and entering the Ligurian Sea to the north. By August 6th, John Monk and the rest of the *Berwick*'s weary boat crews had reached Genoa, where they would remain through to the end of the year.

Back in Gaeta, Begani finally capitulated in late July, when he was informed of Napoleon's surrender to Captain Maitland on the *Bellerophon*.

The conduct of the crews of the *Berwick* and *Malta* during the siege was commended to the Admiralty, and John and the *Berwick*'s other lieutenants were singled out in particular. Lord Exmouth was told in dispatches about the 'Lieutenants of … the *Berwick* who for nearly two months with the exception of a very few nights have in their turn been under the fire of this powerful fortress'.[36]

The *Berwick*'s return to Genoa in August 1815 would have delighted Teresa Massone in particular. She had written to John during the siege at Gaeta to make clear how much she missed him:

I am very angry with this Captain of Gaeta, who detains you here so long time. I pray God to preserve you from every danger, but till this place is not surrendered, I can't be quiet. We have here the Tremendous, *and a frigate of which I don't know the name. I am told that it is that which carried last year that Clever Man Bonaparte in the Island of Elba. But I am acquainted with no English man, and I do nothing to exercise in this tongue, but in teaching it to my young Brothers. Now I want very much so good a Master as you are.*[37]

John and Teresa's father Marcello also exchanged gifts. Marcello gave John an engraved watch and chain, and John, being a man of a practical nature, gave Marcello a stock of pigs. Two years later, his gift had proved its worth. In 1817 the family wrote to John to tell him that the sow had had piglets, and that one of the older pigs had been slaughtered for meat.

Marcello's spiritual home was his country house in Corsanico, about one hundred miles to the south of Genoa, set in the Tuscan countryside. The gardens were extensive, and Marcello was determined to develop them further. During 1816 he spent much of his time there, where he employed a large team of labourers to remodel them, planting three hundred orange and lemon trees and adding a summerhouse for his billiard table. When it was finished, he wrote to John to share his joy:

The view there is delightful, the place larger three times than the old garden, about three hundred lemon and orange trees have been planted in it: everyone who visited it has been pleased and found it beautiful, but I want to have your opinion. I hope I shall have the great pleasure to see you there some day in the bosom of a family to which your memory is always so dear.[38]

Peace in Europe would have been a source of jubilation among the ship's company but also a cause of concern for a junior officer like John, still on the first rung of the commissioned officer ladder. His lieutenant's rank would ensure he received half his pay from the Admiralty between commissions, but opportunities for further progression would be increasingly limited in a time of peace. His hope now would have been for promotion to commander, which would bring him a step closer to the cherished rank of post-captain and the flag officer ranks of admiral that lay beyond.

John would have known that he could take none of this for granted. The Navy had a surfeit of lieutenants, many of whom would never progress above that rank. As a junior officer, without the rock-solid support of a well-connected patron to give influence, John's best hope lay in recognition for gallant deeds and exemplary conduct in combat, much harder to achieve without an enemy to fight. However, there was still one last battle to come for John, and it would prove to be his proudest achievement in active service.

5. Algiers and the *Impregnable*

After Naples surrendered we went against Gaeta, which place we bombarded for two months. After Gaeta surrendered we joined Lord Exmouth and went against Algiers.[1]

The North African states bordering the Mediterranean had long had an uneasy relationship with their European neighbours. The cities of Algiers, Tunis and Tripoli lay along what was known as the Barbary Coast. The power of the Ottoman Empire, of which they were part, had waned since its peak in the sixteenth and seventeenth centuries, but the Barbary states remained a major thorn in the side for the European nations to the north. The problem was the local, highly profitable trade in white European slaves, which had been going on for centuries.

The threat of capture by Barbary pirates or corsairs was a constant danger for sailors in the Mediterranean at this time, as John Monk and every other man on the *Berwick* would have known. It was a worrying prospect. Had John been captured and enslaved, he would have either been sold privately or become the property of the local dey, housed in a large, overcrowded prison and forced to row galleys or to quarry stone. Men or women from wealthy families might be able to buy back their freedom, but most others lived out their lives in slavery, dying of mistreatment, malnourishment or disease.

The pirates did not just operate at sea, but also attacked

European coastal communities. Italy and Spain were the worst hit, but British and Irish prisoners were also taken. By 1815, there were an estimated 49,000 European slaves in the region and in Algiers alone there were said to be a thousand.[2]

During the Napoleonic Wars, Britain's allies in the Mediterranean had been in short supply. The Royal Navy had relied on Algiers and other states for supplies for its Mediterranean bases at Gibraltar and Mahón, but since Napoleon's surrender in 1815, political pressure had grown to rescue the European slaves and to take steps to stop further enslavement.

The British government decided to act and sent Sir Edward Pellew, John Monk's commander-in-chief in the Mediterranean and now Lord Exmouth, on a diplomatic mission to the Barbary states, seeking a pledge to treat Christian captives as prisoners of war rather than slaves. Pellew was given a squadron of six ships of the line for the expedition, one of which was the *Berwick*. The squadron formed at Mahón in March 1816 and made sail to the south.[3]

The mission began well. At an audience with the Dey of Algiers, Omar Pashaw, at the end of March, Pellew negotiated the release of 1,200 men, mainly Neapolitans and Sicilians, in exchange for ransom payments. The squadron headed east for talks with the Dey of Tunis, Mahmoud Pacha. This was a diplomatic mission, but the threat of force was ever-present, and the ships were ordered to exercise their guns when it might assist the tone of negotiations. Pellew achieved his aim and secured a treaty which provided that captured men should be treated as prisoners of war. The third destination for Pellew and his squadron was Tripoli, where meetings with the local dey were also a success, and a further treaty was agreed upon.

Buoyed by his diplomatic successes at Tunis and Tripoli, Pellew decided to return to Algiers, to seek a similar treaty banning the trade in Christian slaves. Unlike his first meetings with the Dey of Algiers, when Pellew's negotiations had involved paying for the release of captured men, this time the stormy discussions did not go so well, as the Dey knew how unpopular a pledge to ban slavery would be with his subjects. There was a prickly, two-day standoff, and hostilities were only averted when the Dey sent a stallion to the admiral and promised that he would refer the question to the Sultan of Turkey. Pellew viewed this as success, and the British squadron left Algiers on May 21st and began their journey back to England.

Unfortunately, news of the Dey's promise travelled slowly. A week later, Algerian soldiers carried out an order issued prior to the agreement and attacked Corsican, Sardinian and Sicilian fishing boats lying under British protection in the port of Bona, now Annaba, in Northern Algeria. More than 150 civilians were killed, the attacks ceasing only when the Dey's messenger belatedly arrived with news of the agreement with Pellew.

Before John arrived back in Plymouth on July 2nd, news of the 'atrocities at Bona' had already reached Britain and Europe.[4] Pellew found that his negotiations were seen as a failure, and the Admiralty immediately ordered him back to sea to punish the Algerians. The time for diplomacy had passed.

For John, the return to Algiers offered something new. The Royal Navy had spent the ten years since Trafalgar enforcing Britain's hard-won naval superiority across the seas of Europe, rather than winning it afresh. John would have understood the importance of blockade duty, support for land troops, and enforcing the economic embargo, but none of these roused the hearts of the British public like the heroic victories at the Nile, Trafalgar or Cape St Vincent.

The problem for John and other ambitious junior officers during the latter stages in the war was that it was the larger actions that provided the greatest opportunity to gain the attention of the Admiralty. The mission to Algiers in 1816 finally offered this. John was to be part of a large-scale action, led by one of the nation's most prestigious admirals. That the slaves held in Algiers were Christian lent the expedition a crusade-like quality. It promised the roar of pounding broadsides, the heat of battle and, most importantly of all, Glory.

Pellew hurriedly assembled a squadron of five ships of the line. He persuaded a weary Captain Brace to take command of the ninety-eight-gun second-rate three-decker, HMS *Impregnable*, and John Monk, now 25 years old, volunteered to join him.[5] The lieutenant and his captain had served together on HMS *Berwick* since 1812 and it had, of course, been Brace who had given John his commission. Just as John had been loyal to Macnamara earlier in his career, so he would be to Brace.

The squadron was being assembled at great speed. Brace, John, and other officers from the *Berwick* came on board HMS *Impregnable* on July 10th, 1816, just a week after arriving back in England from the Mediterranean and without a day's shore leave. Brace set about finding men to join his ship's company and appointed John to prepare the *Impregnable* for foreign duty. The next day the pilot guided the ship the short distance to a mooring near Drake's Island, where, for the next two weeks,

John made the ship ready for sea and for the likely hostilities ahead.

John referred to this interlude later in life, in a summary of his active service:

On our arrival in England the latter end of June 1816 we heard of the dreadful atrocities of Bona. Lord Exmouth was ordered out. I volunteered again with Captain Brace (which officer I had now been with for six years). I was appointed by Captain Brace to commission the Impregnable. *I was ordered to take her out into the Sound, to station the crew and to fit her out with all dispatch for Foreign Service.* [6]

Finding enough men to crew the five ships presented a challenge. Some were brought over by Brace from the *Berwick* and more were received from HMS *Leander* and other ships, but it was still not enough. Many seamen had wanted to leave the Navy at the end of the war with France, and Pellew had to be creative in how he found sufficient numbers. He approached the prisons and offered positions to convicted poachers and smugglers, and took the unusual step of offering to pay his men in advance.[7] On July 22nd the pay clerk duly came on board and paid John Monk and the rest of the ship's company two months wages.

The *Impregnable* set sail for Gibraltar on July 28th, along with the rest of Pellew's assembled fleet. In addition to the five large ships of the line, there were smaller vessels and empty transports ready to carry rescued slaves. On the *Impregnable*, John was to have command of the lower gun deck in the coming conflict. As soon as the fleet was at sea, he and the other officers led their gun crews through round after round of intensive training exercises. John had to make sure that his gun crews could load, fire and reload their guns fast enough to be effective in battle.

The small squadron spent a week in Gibraltar, where each ship was allocated a gunboat. Rear-admiral Milne, second-in-command to Pellew, hoisted his flag on board the *Impregnable*. The fleet was strengthened by six Dutch frigates, and on the morning of August 14th they sailed for the north African coast.

As the sun rose on the morning of Tuesday, August 27th, the fleet was lying off Algiers. This was John Monk's third visit to the city in six months. The city in front of him was stone built, well defended and presented a formidable target. In total, up to a thousand armaments protected the harbour. On his earlier diplomatic visits, John would have noted the huge guns, much heavier than the British ships could carry, which stared back from the city's walls. Below the walls lay the city's harbour, sheltered by a jetty or 'mole', formed by a small island linked to the mainland by a breakwater and itself heavily fortified.

Pellew finalised the plan of attack with his captains and officers. He had surveyed the defences of Algiers discreetly on previous visits and believed he had identified a weakness. The five larger ships of the line were to sail in a column formation into an area next to the mole, where Pellew believed they would be so close to the fortifications that they would be below the elevation of the largest of the Algerian guns. At the same time, HMS *Leander* and *Queen Charlotte* were to enter the harbour and burn, sink, or destroy everything they encountered.

During the morning, Pellew sent a written note to the Dey but received no response. Shortly before one p.m., he signalled to the fleet to prepare to engage the enemy. The *Impregnable* moved into position behind HMS *Superb* as the ships approached the city. There was a brief moment of quiet while each side awaited the other's move, followed by the sudden roar of the Algerian guns shortly before three o'clock. Minutes later, the British ships dropped anchor opposite the lighthouse batteries and returned fire.

The bombardment from both sides was fierce and unlike any of the skirmishes or cutting out operations that John had encountered previously. The British ships mounted wave after wave of broadsides at the fortifications and into the city beyond, and the large Algerian guns pounded the ships relentlessly. The noise of these broadsides was immense. A midshipman on the *Impregnable* wrote later that,

It is impossible to describe the heat and fury of the cannonade. For the first hour, it was dreadful, and deprived me of my hearing; but I recovered it shortly after, and soon got used to the work... The ships company, Officers, men and boys, behaved in a most gallant manner, many of the men near me singing and laughing while the thunder was rattling at them... The whole thing was glorious.[8]

Pellew's strategy had been for his captains to position their ships where they could evade the worst of the destruction. Unfortunately, Brace had miscalculated the *Impregnable*'s position and dropped anchor too early on his approach. Rather than being tucked in beneath the enemy's line of fire like the other British ships, the *Impregnable* and her crew were to be exposed to the full force of the city's huge guns.[9]

The thick oak walls of the *Impregnable* offered little defence against the larger cannon. Danger lay not just in a direct hit but in the explosion of large splinters which each shot could cause as it pierced the ship's hull. At four p.m., the *Impregnable* was rocked by a violent blast which killed and wounded several men. John wrote to his father after the battle and described the scene:

One cruel shot dashed me and fourteen brave fellows down; I was wounded in the knee, though not mentioned in the return; and as soon as I recovered, and cleansed my eyes from the blood, I found ten of my gallant comrades cut to atoms![10]

John's eyes were in a worse state than he had revealed to his father and resulted in the permanent loss of sight in one of them. He would have cause to refer to this in later years as he prepared another summary of his years of active service:

At the bombardment of Algiers, I was wounded in the right thigh (although not reported) and from a heavy explosion of powder my eyes were much injured that I have suffered much from them ever since and the vision of my left eye is now gone.[11]

At four thirty p.m., the *Impregnable*'s launch and boats were sent into the middle of the battle to bombard the town from closer quarters. The Algerian defences were beginning to weaken, and shortly before seven o'clock, a fire broke out among the enemy's ships in the harbour and spread from ship to ship. At eight forty p.m., Captain Brace sent out a barge loaded with barrels of powder, to be run aground below the fortifications. It exploded half an hour later, by which time the city's batteries were almost silent. Every Algerian ship in the harbour was either on fire or had been destroyed and the water was littered with floating bodies.

As evening came, the wind changed and, with a breeze blowing from the shore, Pellew gave the order to make sail and move out of range. Unfortunately for the *Impregnable*, damage to her sails, rigging and mast had left her crippled and unable to manoeuvre. To make matters worse, two enemy ships, both on fire, were drifting out of the harbour and being carried by the breeze towards them. At ten in the evening, a rope was eventually attached to the sloop HMS *Mutine*, which dropped an anchor, and the men on the *Impregnable* were able to haul their way slowly out of danger. By midnight, the battered and bruised *Impregnable* was safely at anchor two miles from the city.

It was raining the morning after the bombardment, but as daylight came, John Monk would have looked out at a scene of destruction. The whole Algerian fleet had burned to the waterline and the city's fortifications had been badly damaged. During the eight hours of the battle, the British and Dutch ships had fired over 50,000 round shot. The *Impregnable* alone had used 480 of her five hundred barrels of gunpowder. Several of the ships had been badly hit, but the *Impregnable* had suffered the heaviest losses, due in part to Brace's navigation error. The British and Dutch had lost 141 lives in total, with 742 wounded, while Algerian casualties were estimated to be in the thousands.[12]

Clearing the ship after the battle could now start, along with the grisly process of tending to the many casualties. John Monk described the scene to his father:

After the firing ceased, it took us the remainder of the night to get our poor shattered ship out; but, good God! As day light appeared, what a horrid and dreadful sight our deck presented! covered over with our dead and wounded comrades...[13]

John had the gruesome duty of clearing the cockpit, gathering up bloody body parts, as the crew began to deal with the carnage around them. The *Chester Courant* on October 1st added a footnote beneath John's account of the battle:

This enterprising young officer collected the shattered limbs of his undaunted comrades and sent up sixteen baskets full to be thrown overboard. He was obliged to have his mouth and nose covered with a handkerchief, dipped in vinegar, during this disagreeable but necessary act.

The ship's carpenter surveyed the damage. The *Impregnable* was the most cut-up of all the ships. Her hull had been holed by 233 large shot, and her masts, sails and rigging were also in very bad shape.[14] The main mast had been hit by eight shot and the foremast by five. The main topmast had been shot away completely. The carpenter's crew began to repair the shot holes they found in the hull and did what they could to secure the damaged masts. The standing and running rigging had been destroyed, so seamen knotted and spliced what remained as best they could. Sailmakers repaired the damage to the sails.

Pellew sent a boat onshore carrying the white flag of truce. It returned during the afternoon, and the admiral's ship signalled to the fleet to confirm that the Dey had agreed to all terms.

The victory was complete, but the fleet had paid a heavy price. On HMS *Impregnable*, the bodies of forty-eight men were commended to the deep on the first day alone. Nearly two hundred more were wounded, many of whom would die in the coming days. The captain's log recorded the death toll as it climbed, and by the time the fleet sailed for Gibraltar a week later, another fourteen men had died as a result of their wounds, infection or the surgeon's hurried amputations.

The journey back to a friendly port would have been a grim one for John. He had seen men killed and wounded on the gun deck while under his command, and he would have been helpless to assist as infections spread among the wounded, as they lay in the dark, humid warmth of the surgeon's bay or the lower decks. Twelve more men died during the week's voyage back to Gibraltar, before the fleet limped into port during the evening of September 11th.

The *Impregnable*'s surgeon had worked tirelessly to save lives and to ease his patients' suffering, and the carpenter had somehow kept the ship afloat, but they were finally able to get the help they desperately needed. Twenty-five men were immediately sent to the hospital and fresh supplies were brought on board for the rest of the weary crew. On her previous visit, the ship had been prepared for battle and stripped of any non-essential comforts. Luggage, stools, bulkheads and provisions were now brought back on board, as life returned to less of a battle footing. One of the most pressing tasks was to replace the badly shot-up main mast. The huge, damaged mast was removed, and a new one was carefully stepped into position.

It was early October by the time John reached Plymouth, where the *Impregnable* would spend much of the next seventy years. There had been four more deaths on board during the journey back to England, including the ship's corporal, a ship's boy and Lieutenant Johnson. The ships of the fleet parted company and HMS *Impregnable* entered Plymouth Sound. Most of the marines were returned to headquarters, and what remained of the ship's company began to strip her down before she entered the dry dock. Each of the heavy guns had to be removed and taken to the gun wharf, along with the remaining gunner's stores and grapeshot. Crew numbers were steadily reduced throughout October. The ship's company was mustered one last time for the clerk of the cheque on Wednesday, October 23rd, before the last of the seamen were either returned to their proper ships or discharged out the service.

A treaty with the Dey was signed in Algiers on September 24th, three weeks after John's sailed from the city. Over a thousand European slaves were freed, restitution was paid, and peace was made between Algiers and the Dutch. The Dey also undertook to abolish slavery, an unpopular pledge that resulted in his murder not long after.

News of Pellew's victory and the slaves' release was greeted with delight by the British press and public, although the attacks by Barbary pirates would only stop properly with the conquest of Algiers by the French in 1830. Awards and promotions were showered on admirals and captains, and particularly on wounded officers, who had put their lives at risk for such a noble cause. Historian William James, writing in *The Naval History of Great Britain*, included a long list of the dead and wounded on each ship present at Algiers and ended his account with details of the accolades given to British officers on their return:

For the skill and valour he had displayed in consummating this glorious achievement, Lord Exmouth was created a viscount of the United Kingdom. Rear-admiral Milne, also, was made a knight-commander, and captains Ekins, Aylmer, Wise, Maitland, Paterson, and Coode, companions, of the Bath. All the lieutenants named in the list in the preceding page, and some others including lieutenant Fleming who commanded the explosion vessel, were promoted to the rank of commanders; and several of the master's mates and midshipmen obtained commissions as lieutenants. [15]

Two familiar names are noticeably absent from this honours list, although each had been wounded during the battle. According to John Marshall's *Royal Naval Biography,*

Captain Brace himself was slightly wounded in two places but, as he did not allow his name to be included in the report, we suppose it was not his wish to make a longer list than he could possibly avoid of the casualties on board his ship. The names of... one or two other officers who received wounds, were probably withheld through the same motive. Such acts of modesty are truly praiseworthy, and should always be recorded.[16]

John had seemingly followed his captain's lead and not allowed either the wound to his right thigh or the damage to one eye to be declared in the report to the Admiralty. If the course of a life can be said to pivot on a handful of often minor decisions, then this, for John, was one of them. As the honours and promotions were handed out by a grateful nation to all those wounded officers, the absence of his name from the Admiralty list may have been an omission that John came to regret.

The Bombardment of Algiers remained a source of pride throughout John's long life. Each year on August 27th, the anniversary of the battle, newspapers published an ever-shorter list of surviving officers who had been part of 'Lord Exmouth's great victory'.[17] On that same day each year, John's neighbours could see him in his garden in Parkgate Road, solemnly raising a flag to commemorate those who had fallen during the battle.[18]

By the end of the war with France, the Royal Navy had far more ships and men in active service than were now required in peacetime and, with the country facing bankruptcy after the costly war, the Admiralty had undertaken a vast and rapid reduction in size. Ships of the line were expensive to maintain and to keep seaworthy, and many were quickly taken out of service. Of these, some were readied to be kept 'in ordinary'. Sails, rigging and fittings were removed, before what remained entered long-term mooring in harbours like Chatham until a day when they might again be required.

Two of the four naval ships on which John had served were broken up shortly after peace with France. HMS *Berwick*, never her sailing master's favourite, had the shortest life and was sent to join many others of the Forty Thieves at the breakers yard in 1821. HMS *Dictator* had seen service throughout the long war and was broken up in 1817. The future had different things in store, though, for HMS *Edgar* and HMS *Impregnable*.

HMS *Edgar* was the seventy-four-gun third-rate ship of the line which had been the sometimes-leaky home to midshipman John Monk in the Baltic between 1808 and 1809. She had seen service throughout the American Revolutionary, French Revolutionary and Napoleonic Wars, but the years after the war took her from being the pride of England to a source of fear and hatred. She was converted into a prison hulk in 1814 and renamed *Retribution*. All the features that had once allowed her to sail - the rigging, masts and rudder - were removed and the internal structure was reconfigured to create prison cells.

These floating prisons were widely dreaded. They had initially been approved by Parliament in 1776 as a temporary measure but remained in use much longer than originally intended, despite repeated campaigns to have them banned as inhumane. In 1833, the *Retribution*, the rotting shadow of a once-proud ship that had fought in the battles of Cape St Vincent and

Copenhagen, was finally towed to Deptford and broken up.

HMS *Impregnable* had been built in Chatham in 1810, just six years before Lieutenant John Monk's final active service at the bombardment of Algiers, where she had been nearly destroyed. After modifications and repairs, the *Impregnable* spent much of the next four decades moored in Devonport, Plymouth with the reserve fleet, although there were interludes where she took the role of flagship in Portsmouth harbour in 1839 and where she made a brief return to the Mediterranean.

The old wooden ship was given a new lease of life in 1862 and spent the next twenty-four years as a training ship moored at Devonport for boys joining the Navy. Many of these boys were orphans or street urchins, ordered onto the training ship by a magistrate, while others were unruly children, sent away by their parents. In 1886, the *Impregnable* was replaced as the Devonport training ship by HMS *Hood*, which was renamed HMS *Impregnable* in her honour. After being decommissioned as a training ship, the old *Impregnable* spent three years as HMS *Kent*, intended for use in the event of an epidemic.

In 1891, the ageing ship was again renamed, this time to HMS *Caledonia*, and sailed north to the Forth of Firth, off Port Edgar, where she resumed her role as a training ship. Finally, in 1906, aged 96, she was taken out of service and broken up. Her timbers are still in use today, supporting the cloister of St Conan's Kirk, next to Loch Awe.[19]

Back in Genoa, Marcello Massone's concern for John's safety had grown when he learned that he was to be part of the attack on Algiers, and he shared his delight at the news of John's safe return. The victory was made real for the family when a freed slave called Badaracco returned home from Tunis, full of praise for the navy that had given him back his freedom, all of which raised John still higher in the Massones' estimation:

I begin this letter to you, giving thanks to God Almighty who heard the prayers I addressed to him very often since your departure from England. I was frightened indeed when I knew from your dear letter of 16ᵗʰ July that you were appointed to the expedition of Algiers, for I foresaw what happened: and you may suppose my daily uneasiness on your account... I was informed that you are safe and very well. I was then overjoyed and happy as I was when my dear Mark was recovered from his illness, and I think to have got again two lost Sons in the same year. I read with horror the account of the dreadful battle you fought.[20]

A lieutenant on half-pay, 1817

Algiers would represent John Monk's final active duty for the Royal Navy, but eight years would pass before his next career move, as the Navy and its officers adjusted to a new and unfamiliar period of peace. For John, it would be a period marked by indecision, despondency and the occasional society ball.

John was discharged on half-pay in October 1816. He had been away at sea for the best part of ten years, returning only for short spells when granted shore leave. Returning once more to his family in Parkgate, he would have seen changes not just in his immediate family but also in the community from which he had been largely absent for the past decade.

The news from his father William about his work with the customs service would have been bleak, although perhaps not unexpected. The Dee estuary's deep-water channel had shifted away from the Wirral and closer to Wales, and the waters around Parkgate had slowly silted up until its port could no longer be entered. The last recorded boat to land passengers at Parkgate had been in 1812.[21] William remained as senior customs officer until his retirement in 1823; unsurprisingly, his role was not replaced. The village's popularity with sea bathers would also suffer as the sand banks rose. Before long, the estuary waters would only reach the sea wall at high tide. The rest of the time, bathers were left high and dry.

The end of the long war meant that John could finally enjoy some of the pleasures of Georgian society and appreciate the esteem in which naval officers were generally held. Chester was a thriving, wealthy city with a busy social calendar, and newspapers confirm his attendance at several events in the first years of peace.

In January 1818, John joined four hundred other guests at the Royal Hotel Chester for a ball thrown by the Grosvenor family for their son Robert, who had recently returned from the Continent where he had undertaken his Grand Tour. Guests danced until midnight, after which dinner was served across several sittings in two rooms. Among the guests was a Miss Russell, possibly the same young lady whom John would later come close to marrying.

October 1821 saw John attend a charity musical festival at Chester Cathedral along with the Archbishop of York and members of the gentry. Political rivals the Grosvenor and Egerton families were both present, although not necessarily on the same day. The *Chester Courant* was glowing in its praise for the occasion but damning of some of the performances. 'We believe there never was an occasion on which the city of Chester was honoured with such an influx of distinguished personages; nor did our capacious cathedral ever contain so much beauty, elegance, and fashion.' Criticism of the performances included that of Mr Rolle who 'has a fine, mellow-toned voice, and... would do very well if he could be kept from going to sleep'.[22]

It was a rare luxury to spend time with friends and family but, longer term, John knew he had some decisions to make. Peace had come at an unfortunate time for an ambitious young officer, and his prospects were now uncertain. He could be patient and hope for a future commission from the Admiralty, or he could make other plans. He was still a young man and could not live indefinitely on the meagre half-pay of a lieutenant and his accumulated prize money. He had joined the Navy aged fourteen and would have known little else. He was blind in one eye after the gunpowder explosion at Algiers and his body carried the aches and pains of war.

Unlike some of his peers, John's family were sufficiently affluent to mean he did not need to fear the spiralling debt into which others would fall. However, events in John's life show that he was a proud, even stubborn, man, who would have been unwilling to depend either upon the financial support of his ageing father or the generosity of his rather uptight eldest brother, Charles.

Martin Wilcox, in his paper *These Peaceable Times Are the Devil*, highlights how bleak the outlook could be for a junior officer in John's position.[23] Many lieutenants lived for years on their half-pay, hoping for a further naval commission, frustrated by the enforced idleness but unable to find employment elsewhere. Others moved into associated careers, often linked to the sea. Some found posts as harbour masters or with the coast guard. Others returned to the water on revenue cutters or with the Post Office packet service.

The obvious direction was to move into the merchant service, as naval personnel had traditionally done in times of peace. For John, in particular, a history of merchant shipping ran through generations of his mother's family. His grandfather, John Matthews, had captained the *Minerva* for many years between Parkgate and Dublin, and his great-aunt Mary had married into another of Neston's seafaring families, the Ryders. Her husband Stephen Ryder sailed from Parkgate as captain of the *Prince of Wales*, and in turn, their sons Stephen and John Ryder also captained privateers and merchant vessels.

Although a transition from His Majesty's Navy to the merchant service would not have been a step entirely into the unknown for John, such a move was not straightforward. The Royal Navy had discharged thousands of men between 1813 and 1817, many of whom, officers among them, would have expected to turn to the merchant service for further employment, but found instead that their services were not required. Decades of war had left Great Britain's finances in tatters, and a severe agricultural and commercial depression had led to high unemployment. The merchant service would recover in time, to the point where, by 1840, forty percent of the world's trade was British, but in the years immediately after the Treaty of Paris in 1815, the industry was in a slump.[24] For John to move into the merchant service in this climate, especially if he were to invest in a share of a vessel, carried significant financial risk.

John may also have met with doubts from other mariners when he first explored this possibility. Many merchant masters looked down on naval officers because the Navy's ships were so heavily over-crewed. The large size of a naval ship's company was determined by the need to man the ship's guns in action. Outside of battle, though, there were always dozens of men on hand to assist, haul on ropes and generally act as muscle where needed. In contrast, a merchant vessel had to run as a business. Crews could be no larger than required, as each additional head further reduced the profit to the captain or owners. Royal Navy seamen might brag about how quickly they could make and take in sail, but merchant seamen would counter that they could do the same with a tenth of the men.

The rivalry was strong. Early in his working life, Horatio Nelson spent a year on a merchantman, *Mary Ann*, travelling to Tobago and Jamaica, while his uncle, Maurice Suckling, sought to establish whether this rather sickly child was suited to service at sea. Nelson later remarked about this voyage,

I returned a practical seaman, with a horror of the Royal Navy... It was many weeks before I got in the least reconciled to a man-of-war, so deep was the prejudice rooted.[25]

One path that John appears to have discounted was to follow his father and his brothers, Charles and Joseph, into the customs service. John had his hopes pinned to adventures further afield.

By 1820, eldest brother Charles was the superintendent of quarantine at Bromborough Pool in the Port of Liverpool. He was captain of the guard brig *Red-breast*, which was used to protect the valuable cargo that might be in storage on the two quarantine ships. Among Charles's team was his brother

Joseph, captain of the *Experiment*. The ship had previously been a forty-four-gun frigate before she was decommissioned and converted into a floating lazaretto, or quarantine station, on a fixed mooring. Joseph had a crew of eleven under his command, although in John's eyes they were probably more akin to dockers and guards than real seamen.

Joseph's position was one of responsibility and trust. Merchants worried that their precious goods, especially silk, might be stolen or damaged during the quarantine process. To prevent this, their cargo was weighed on arrival and departure, and the quarantine ship was not allowed to have boats of her own. Charles's guard-brig was his brother's main source of contact with the outside world.

Charles married Elizabeth Jones in 1818. They made their home at the Hermitage, a characterful Regency villa on Parkgate Road, built around the time of their wedding. The house still stands today, largely untouched by later modification. Gothic arches sit atop each of the large sash windows and, at the rear, a wide veranda runs the length of the house, with a lattice frame to support rambling rose bushes. Charles's name remains in the window where he scratched it in 1823.

Charles appears from surviving records to have been of an earnest and serious-minded disposition, more so than his younger brothers. He was the landowner in the family, with a sizeable portfolio of properties and farmland. While brothers John and Joseph owned fields locally, they seem to have remained as residential tenants of their brother. The picture of exactly where each of them lived in Parkgate Road is further confused by the self-deprecating fashion of referring to every house as 'the cottage'.

Their youngest brother, Whitehouse, led a short, troubled life, and was undoubtedly the black sheep in a family of naval captains, private pews and good regard in the community. In an expensive foray into business in 1819, he became the landlord of the Ermine Inn in Flookersbrook, Chester. He had lofty ambitions for the place, and advertised that,

No exertion shall be wanting to render the House in every respect comfortable and to keep a constant supply of GOOD GRASS, together with a stock of the very best HOME BREWED BEER.[26]

Unfortunately though, ambition was not matched by business acumen. The venture was a disaster and by 1826 Whitehouse's life was falling apart. He was an alcoholic, bankrupt and arguing with his creditors. His wife Hannah was ill and close to death, his youngest son was small and sickly, and his daughter Bess had been sent to live with her grandparents in Parkgate. He was also facing the ire of his parents and siblings. Among his creditors was his father William, who stood to lose £700 (roughly £40,000 in today's money) and, to make matters worse, he had borrowed a further £500 from his brother Charles, at a point where he had already known that his business was in trouble. He faced prison unless he could persuade his family to reach an agreement with his creditors.[27]

Joseph commented to his sister Elizabeth, in a parting shot of exasperation at their brother,

What has become of all the money God only knows... It is strange, the man that's taken Whitehouse's house is doing as much business as he wishes and quite surprised that Whitehouse lost money there.[28]

After his wife Hannah died in 1827, Whitehouse seems to have given up on life. He found work where he could, as a clerk at his brother-in-law John Brown's auction house and then as a journeyman to a mill in Chester, but his mental decline continued during the next decade. Finally, in February 1836, his brother Charles co-signed a letter declaring that Whitehouse was of 'unsound mind', and he was admitted to the recently-opened Chester Asylum, where he died two weeks later, aged just 41.[29]

In 1817, John Monk contacted his former captain Edward Brace, under whose command he had served on the *Berwick* and the *Impregnable*, to ask advice on his future direction.

In his response, Brace bemoaned his own lack of employment and was circumspect in his words to John. He suggested that he should be patient and look for the right opportunity, but also recognised that as a young man it might be better for John to 'keep afloat'. Brace noted that the 'chance of war is... far distant, and the prospect of employment equally so for me'. Brace offered encouragement but no practical assistance, admitting that he had used much of his influence to promote the career of his nephew, Francis:[30]

The command of a ship to India might be very well, and more useful than an idle life, which brings on bad habits, not easy to be got rid of, but until anything offered that was advantageous, I should direct my attention to study and the improvement of the mind.

One reason Brace recommended to John that he should keep busy was to assist his claim for promotion to commander, explaining that 'it establishes, together with your former exertions, a claim in the service, that must ultimately be attended to'. If John could indeed achieve the promotion that he sought, his financial prospects would be much improved. His income as a captain would be more comfortable and in time he could expect to be promoted to rear-admiral, even if he never set foot on a ship again, as the Navy operated a system of automatic promotion, but this did not apply to lieutenants.

It was common after significant naval victories for the Admiralty to promote officers shown to have acquitted themselves well, as John felt he had. He watched as officers on other ships present at Algiers were promoted to commander or post-captain, and complained in letters to friends that even the small brigs had seen their officers promoted. A rumour had spread that there was to be a large round of promotions in June 1816, on the anniversary of the Battle of Waterloo, but this milestone came and went without the promotion for which John had hoped.

Captain Brace had good reason to be gloomy about his own prospects. While John had been overlooked when honours and promotions were distributed, Captain Brace had been pointedly excluded, in the face of criticism for his costly navigation mistake at Algiers and the resulting death toll on his ship. By November 1816, Brace had decamped from the *Impregnable* to Surrey Street, London and watched, like John, as other officers were rewarded. He wrote to the Lords of the Admiralty on November 25th, in messy, hurried handwriting, clearly upset at the humiliating snub. He reminded the Lords of his many years' service and asked them to consider his career in the round:

I have to express a hope that their Lordships will be pleased to take the same into consideration, and place me on a footing with those junior officers, who have been advanced to honours over my head, so that I may feel a sense of their Lordships' justice.[31]

Not to be swayed, but appreciating the sensitivity of the matter, Lord Melville informed the Board that he would answer Captain Brace privately. The injustice that Brace was feeling also extended to other officers on his ship. Brace himself wrote to the Admiralty complaining that only one midshipman on the *Impregnable* had been promoted, the same number as on each of the smaller vessels, 'who bore but a slight part in that severe battle in which the *Impregnable* suffered so much'. Recognition is more easily given for success than for suffering.

Edward Brace's reputation would be slow to recover. He continued to face criticism for his error and was reputedly judged by one contemporary historian as being 'blessed with neither great ability nor great intellect'.[32] He had joined the Navy as a boy of twelve and had been in service for most of the time since. He had married in Brockhampton in 1800, although his wife Elizabeth was long since dead. He had no children of his own but was close to his nephew, Francis, who often served under him, and whose departure from the *Berwick* had helped pave the way for John Monk's own rise to lieutenant in 1814.

Brace did indeed return to service in 1821, but his days in the distant seas of the Caribbean or Mediterranean were behind him. He commanded guard-ships in the Downs and Portsmouth Harbour, before promotion to rear-admiral in 1830 and to vice-admiral in 1838. His death came in Sheerness in 1841, while serving as commander-in-chief of the Nore, with his nephew Francis as his flag captain. The ceremonial aspects of his funeral were in keeping with the passing of a senior officer, but press reports of his death were generally brief and turned quickly to speculation about who might be next to receive his sizable salary.

The uncertainty John faced about his future employment was common among men who had served during the war. Within the family, John's cousin Richard would have found himself in a similar position. He had had a busy war and had been actively engaged during the Peninsular War and later in Belgium. After promotion from ensign to lieutenant with the Royal Cheshire Militia in 1812, he volunteered into the 22nd (Cheshire) Regiment in 1813. As the war approached its conclusion, Richard served as paymaster in the Brunswick Oels corps, commonly nicknamed the Black Brunswickers, due to their distinctive black uniforms and silvered death's head badges. His regiment was heavily engaged in the battle of Quatre Bras, and days later, at Waterloo on June 18th, Wellington held the weary Brunswickers back until the latter stages of the battle, where they launched counterattacks on the French cavalry.

In the months that followed, Richard was praised for his bravery at Waterloo and received promotion to captain, as the *Chester Chronicle* reported:

Mr. Richard Monk, Paymaster of the Duke of Brunswick Oels Corps of Huzzars, is promoted to a Captaincy for the bravery displayed in several actions in the late war, and particularly at the battle of Waterloo.[33]

Like his cousin, Richard spent the first few years after the war on half-pay, but whereas John struggled to secure a new naval commission in peacetime, Richard was able to continue his active service with the army. Now Captain Richard Monk, he served with the 53rd (Shropshire) Regiment from 1818 and, by January 1825, he held the post of paymaster with the 31st (Huntingdonshire) Regiment, with whom he served in the East Indies, a position that would prove to be his last.

Friendships can come about through all manner of unexpected encounters, as John had already seen after his rescue of the young Teresa Massone. In March 1820, John's involvement in a different rescue, on the Old Dee Bridge at Chester, led to a friendship with Richard Grosvenor, the 2nd Marquess of Westminster and the wealthiest man in the country. The story of how they met shines a light on the murky world of Georgian politics.

The city of Chester had two seats in Parliament at the time, both held unopposed by the Grosvenor family for many years. It was democracy of sorts, but the system had evolved to maintain the status quo. In more recent years, though, the Grosvenors' dominance had increasingly been challenged. Candidates representing the city's mercantile and manufacturing interests began to stand as Independents, the most prominent being the Egerton family. Elections were fiercely contested, often with ugly scenes.[34]

On Saturday evening, March 11th, 1820, the Grosvenor and Egerton candidates had each been speaking at hustings. Speeches had ended and the crowds were dispersing. Richard Grosvenor's cousin, General Thomas Grosvenor, the family's second candidate, was heading back to Eaton Hall. His carriage reached the narrow, medieval Old Dee Bridge, just as it was being crossed by a crowd of his rival John Egerton's supporters, with John Monk and his brother among them.

For reasons that were later disputed, rather than waiting for the road to clear, the general's carriage and four horses were driven at speed into the crowd. Pedestrians crossing the narrow bridge were unable to get out of the way in time, many were knocked down and several were injured. An angry mob retaliated, freed the horses and began to heave the carriage and its occupants over the side of the bridge. John, his brother and several others saw what was about to happen and, after a scuffle, managed to open the carriage door and drag the General and his counsellor from their carriage, just as it was tipped over the side of the bridge, smashing to pieces twenty-five feet below. They led the General to safety at a nearby hotel, where he stayed until midnight before finally continuing to Eaton Hall, cut and badly bruised, but alive.

Two days later, on March 13th, 1820, John received a note from General Grosvenor, presenting 'his compliments and best thanks' for 'the kind assistance rendered to him in the unfortunate affair at the Bridge'.[35] A statement released by the General read,

He has to thank many gallant Gentlemen for the services they rendered him and the more particularly many Gentlemen who are opposed to him in the present contest. As for the Old Coach, the Nymphs of the Dee are heartily welcome to it.[36]

The events on the Old Dee Bridge brought John to the attention of a grateful Grosvenor family. Richard Grosvenor, the General's cousin, would be present with John at social engagements around Cheshire in the years that followed, and an enduring friendship would develop between the two men, although not without its disagreements.

With his experience at sea, loyalty to the Wirral and status as a naval officer, John was the ideal person to champion an ambitious, if fanciful, plan to launch a new steam-crossing to Dublin from the village of Dawpool, in preference to Liverpool. Parkgate was no longer accessible, but Dawpool lay further downstream on the banks of the Dee, where the channel was still deep. It is odd now to think of a debate about the merits of this forgotten village over that of mighty Liverpool, but John and his brother-in-law in Dublin, Edward Acton Gibbon, were both consulted as 'very competent authorities' and saw merit in the idea. John spoke eloquently in Dawpool's favour, although history was not with him on this matter:[37]

Dawpool possesses many advantages over Liverpool for Steam Vessels to sail from and to Dublin. For instance, suppose it be high water at the meridian, and each packet is to sail at AM, the Liverpool Packet would have a very strong tide to contend with for four hours, perhaps a breeze of wind, or heavy seas. The Dawpool Packet, sailing at the same hour, would have little tide, no sea, being inside instead of outside of Hoyle...

A test run in August 1823 seemed to confirm John's view, when a steamship completed the journey from Dawpool to Dublin in an impressive time into a strong headwind. Nonetheless, the scheme found no financial backers and proceeded no further.

The letters from the Massone family in Genoa continued to arrive at Parkgate Road, but the news they brought was often troubled and the outlook increasingly grim. Marcello, who had taken such delight in his home at Corsanico, was horrified to find his newly planted citrus orchard under threat in

1818, when the military proposed to build a road to Genoa and Spezia running close to the house and across his beloved gardens. Massone objected and lodged complaints but with little hope of success.

Marcello wrote that the mood in Genoa had initially been merry when the British liberated the city, but Italy was now in the middle of a humanitarian crisis. The region had been hit by a prolonged drought. Crops had failed, famine was widespread, and epidemics of smallpox and other diseases were sweeping through the population. Although the poor were always worst affected, disease also reached the Massone family. Marcello's son Marco was taken ill with smallpox in 1816. Several years later he was still weak on his legs and unable to walk far:

You cannot imagine how the distress is great here in the low people. Famine, misery, want of labour, military conscriptions as in the time of war, taxes and every unpleasant thing have been the consequences of our passage from the state of war to that of peace. I don't know, or rather I cannot say what is the cause of it: but I can assure you that everyone is extremely unsatisfied and complaining more than it was in the old dreadful times. So, the City is not at all so merry as it was when the English troops took possession of it.[38]

Marcello's affection for John was undoubtedly genuine but also potentially very useful to him, as he strove to help his children to get ahead in life. Marcello shared with John that his son Marco showed little interest in following his father into Law and was more interested in the merchant business. The opportunity to send Marco to Great Britain, such a powerful trading nation, could have been invaluable.

Several years would pass before John returned to Italy, although he continued to correspond with the Massones, whether from his home in Parkgate or from Dublin where he often stayed with his sister Elizabeth. Having decided that John was now his adopted English son, Marcello felt able to scold him for not writing regularly. At other times, letters and parcels got lost in transit, and Marcello was left to thank John for gifts that had not yet arrived. Marcello was proud of the oranges, lemons and olive oil that his garden produced and was keen to send some to John and his relatives via Liverpool.

John Monk's letters to the Admiralty during this period are all held among the ADM papers at The National Archives. Most are mundane requests for leave of absence but together they paint a slightly restless portrait. John's hopes of a future with the Royal Navy are slowly fading, and other ideas begin to creep in. Each ends with his distinctive signature, the letters leaning to the right, with a looped line underneath and two dots in the centre, like a miniature pig's snout. One letter from 1820 shows that John hoped to be appointed as an officer on the Northern Expedition, William Parry's second voyage through the ice and islands north of Canada, in search of the fabled North-West Passage from the Atlantic to the Pacific. John would not have been alone in chasing such a position, and many half-pay officers applied to the Admiralty each time they learned ships were being fitted out. John wrote to state his case but, after a long wait, the reply came that all necessary officers had been appointed.[39]

By February 1821, after nearly four years without a commission, John decided it was time to return to Genoa and visit his Italian family. He obtained a year's leave from the Admiralty, and sailed from Liverpool, most likely in March, spending up to three months in Italy. There may also have been more to this voyage than John admitted to the Admiralty. Although willing to grant leave to officers moving into the merchant service, the Admiralty tended to frown on naval officers taking roles considered beneath their station.[40] It would be another three years before John would command his first merchant vessel, and this voyage to Genoa in 1821 is likely to have served as fact finding. Rather than admit to a more junior position such as mate, John may have felt it more prudent simply to present it to his naval employer as a leisure trip.

John sailed from Genoa before the heat of the Italian summer became unbearable and was back in Dublin by August, visiting Elizabeth, her husband Edward and their children. Born in 1779, Elizabeth was ten years older than John and had moved to Dublin while John was still a boy of 12. The two were close, though, and through a mix of circumstance and affection, they would see a lot of each other through the years.

His brother-in-law Edward was well placed to give John advice on his future plans, with two decades of experience working with the merchant service. Previously a shipping agent, Edward was now employed as the Supervisor of Ballast Lighters and Pay Clerk for the Ballast Office, which controlled the Port of Dublin. Although not at sea himself, there would have been few people in the city with a clearer view of the workings of the industry.

The voyage to Genoa in 1821 may not have been John's first return to the Mediterranean, although the evidence of another visit does not lie in The National Archives. Seventy years after John's period of indecision about whether to join the merchant service, his nephew, William Brown, was invited to the Isle of

Man. It was 1889 and William stood in Peel's Centenary Hall before an enthusiastic audience, and gave a speech about his late uncle, who had given his name to the town's lifeboat. Among William's anecdotes, one of the most intriguing involved John's brush with the pirate, Charles Delano.

The last pirate in the waters of the Mediterranean, upon one occasion when John Monk's vessel was at Leghorn, laid by with the intention of committing piracy upon her, but he found that she had the heels of him, and instead he committed piracy upon the vessel of Captain Cornish, and was hung for it at Malta. [41]

William was giving a second-hand account of events more than a half century earlier, and placing John in the Mediterranean at this time has proved hard to do, but if events unfolded as William described, then John was fortunate to have evaded Delano's brig, as the brutal attack that followed nearly cost Captain Cornish and his crew their lives...

Charles Christopher Delano was master of the brig *William*, which had sailed from Liverpool on July 18th, 1819, bound first for Malta and then for Smyrna (modern-day İzmir). Delano was a proficient mariner but had seemingly become consumed by bitterness after an earlier smuggling conviction. As he sailed towards the Mediterranean, he plied his crew with rum and laid before them his plan to capture a vessel. Foolishly the crew backed him and drunkenly shouted that they wanted a 'short life and a merry one', something the majority would achieve, at least in part.

The would-be pirates found what they had been looking for when they spotted the *Helen*, captain Richard Cornish, underway to Genoa. Having painted over their brig's name and built an imitation wooden cannon, they were ready to put their plan into action. They drew in close to their prize, where Delano fired his musket and threatened to sink her. Cornish and his crew were forced down into the *Helen*'s forecastle and the hatch was nailed shut, after which the pirates set about transferring the cargo of woollen and cotton goods back to the *William*. Their final acts were to destroy the *Helen*'s longboat and water pump, and to drill large holes in her hull beneath the waterline, intending that she would sink without trace and take her trapped crew down into the depths.

Delano and his men sailed on for Malta and arrived at the capital Valletta on August 29th, where they found buyers for some of the stolen goods before sailing for Smyrna to sell the rest.

Back on the *Helen*, as the water rose around them, the prisoners found an axe in the dark and managed to smash their way through the hatch and back onto deck. They escaped into the badly damaged longboat and kept her afloat through constant bailing for just long enough to be rescued by a Greek brig, which put them ashore at Cadiz. Unfortunately for Delano, two of Cornish's rescued men travelled on to Malta. From the descriptions they gave of their attacker, it was immediately clear that she was the *William*. The seamen followed Delano to Smyrna aboard HMS *Frederick* and arrived in time to see their attackers arrested.

By the time the trial began on January 27th, 1820, two of Delano's men had volunteered to give evidence and escaped prosecution. The rest appeared before a grand jury where, after a three-day hearing, they were all pronounced guilty and sentenced to death by hanging in a macabre fashion reserved for Maltese pirates.[42]

Delano's brig was painted black and towed to the middle of

the harbour before the execution. Large crowds watched as the men were rowed out to their brig where they were hanged. The corpses were then cut down and taken to nearby Fort Ricasoli at the entrance to the harbour, where the bodies of Delano and three others were placed in individual iron cages hanging from gibbets, with the rest buried beneath them.

Seven years later, in 1827, a visitor to Valletta noted in his diary that the remains of Delano and the others were still swinging in the wind:

...the spectacle of four pirates hung in chains, who were executed several years ago, and have remained on their gibbets ever since. They are kept there in terrorem — as scarecrows... Nothing can be more hideous, especially when the wind is high, than to behold, even from a distance, those carcasses in their tattered coverings, dangling to the breeze.[43]

John would have known Richard Cornish personally in the years that followed. Both men commanded merchantmen sailing from Liverpool on Mediterranean routes through the 1820s and 1830s, and both shared George Yates as their agent. Their sailing schedules sometimes aligned, and Yates would advertise their calls for cargo side by side in *Gore's Liverpool General Advertiser*. It is easy to imagine John the storyteller feeling a twinge of envy that his friend had been at the centre of such drama. [44]

John's indecision continued. Six years had passed since he had last seen active service at the Bombardment of Algiers, but, in 1822, he still seems to have been undecided about joining the merchant service in some capacity. John wrote to Marco Massone and described his situation. Peacetime opportunities for young officers were limited but his hopes were briefly lifted by the worsening political situation in the Eastern Mediterranean. Greek revolutionaries had declared war on Turkey and the Ottoman Empire in 1821. The eastern Mediterranean was facing a period of turbulence, with the possibility of Britain entering the war in support of Greece. Giving a view from the Mediterranean, though, Marco encouraged John to look beyond this:

You begin to think of doing something and you are very right, but the uncertainty we are in about political courses in the Levant keeps you in suspense. I am of opinion that there will be no war, and that you'll perform your project of buying a vessel and come to see us all. How happy should I be if that might happen![45]

Marco encouraged his friend further in this direction, advising on profitable cargo:

The ships that get you a good freight are those which are bound with silk for London: indeed, they remain a long time in the harbour, but at last they are well recompensed. Several ships sailed this year with a cargo of four or five hundred bails of silk each.

Marco's letter of 1822 is the last we hear of the Massones among John's papers, aside from an account of a visit to Genoa many years later by John's niece. As well as offering advice on shipping, Marco also brought him up to date on family news. Teresa, once so besotted with John, was now happily married to Francesco Pescia and together they ran his family's business, manufacturing silk and velvet. Marco told John that that Teresa had a young son, Filippo, 'the finest boy I ever saw. The tiddler becomes a greater scamp every day'.[46]

6. A voyage on the *William Black*

With the arrival of 1824, John's plans took on fresh clarity. He had secured financial backing for a share of a merchant brig and appeared settled on his intention to work the trade routes from Liverpool to the Mediterranean.

Even now, though, the lingering hope of a naval commission appears to have remained. British newspapers were reporting that several ships were to be commissioned immediately, most likely for the next of Parry's northern expeditions. John wrote to the Admiralty and laid his dilemma before them. He asked whether he could expect a posting and explained that he and his backers were about to make a significant investment that would require a twelve-month commitment. Unable or unwilling to offer any guarantees, the Admiralty granted him the leave he was seeking.[1]

Three months later, aged 33, John made his inaugural voyage as a merchant master on the *William Black*. She was a two-masted brig, built in 1819 in Workington, Cumbria. John's destination was Livorno, the port city on the Tuscan coast. Known to the British as Leghorn, over the centuries the city had become one of the most important ports in the Mediterranean. Its fortunes had suffered during the Napoleonic Wars, when trade with Britain had been prohibited. Most of the English-speaking community had left by the time of Napoleon's first Italian campaign in 1796, but, in the nine years since the end of the war, trading networks had been re-established and

Britain's cultural contact with Tuscany was increasing as writers, artists and travellers began to return to the area.

The difference in size between the *William Black* and the Royal Navy ships on which John Monk had sailed was striking. Everything about HMS *Impregnable* had been on a huge scale. She had three decks, three masts, ninety-eight heavy guns and vast stores of ammunition, gunpowder, provisions and everything else a second-rate ship of the line might need. There had been more than eight hundred lives on board, all working, eating and sleeping in an ordered pattern of roles and routines. Everyone knew their place, seamen and officers, whether they liked it or not. Even the all-powerful captain had his orders from the Admiralty or commander-in-chief.

The *William Black* was tiny in comparison. She was just a third of the length of the *Impregnable*, seventy feet from bow to stern and less than half her width at the waterline. The tons burthen, an antiquated volumetric calculation of her cargo capacity, reveals the true picture, though. The *Impregnable* had a tonnage weight of 2,406 tons, compared to his new brig at just 115 tons. The *William Black* was a twentieth of the size.

John was accompanied on the *William Black* by a crew of eight: a mate, six seamen and an apprentice or ship's boy, all from the Liverpool area. Whether the voyage went smoothly or badly would in large part be down to John as master. He had commercial pressures, investors to keep happy, customers awaiting their cargo, and he had to operate without the support network of the Royal Navy. Every cost or delay would be felt directly by him or his backers. He was now an employer of merchant seamen who voluntarily signed articles to crew his brig, rather than a prison guard of press-ganged men, working with the threat of the lash or court-martial in the background.

The mate on this first voyage, Charles Welsh, would remain a constant for the next six years, sailing with John on each of his trips. Another regular on the *William Black* was John Bethell, who began as the ship's boy and learnt the trade to become a regular seaman. It speaks to John's fair-handed treatment of his crew that so many of the same men chose to return for later voyages.

John and his crew sailed the *William Black* out of Liverpool on April 5th, 1824, allowing them to benefit from the warmer spring and summer weather. John knew the route south well from his years with the Royal Navy and made good time. A month later, on May 5th, they were at anchor at Leghorn.

The journey from port to port could take anywhere between three to six weeks depending on the weather. An advert for a later voyage proudly announced that the *William Black* had arrived in Leghorn from Liverpool after 'a fine passage of 24 days'.[2] On the other hand, if the wind died down and the brig was becalmed, she could remain almost stationary for several days.

Some of John's time on land would have been spent with agents and merchants, planning for the return leg of the journey and building connections, but he would also have had time to relax and socialise. His relationship with Italy was already strong. Ten years earlier, as a lieutenant on HMS *Berwick* during the war with Napoleon's nephew Murat and the Kingdom of Naples, John had blockaded or bombarded many of the ports he was now to visit in times of peace. Ahead of each voyage, John wrote a near-identical letter to inform the Admiralty that he required six or twelve months leave of absence as he intended to visit Leghorn and Genoa. Leghorn for business, where his brig could dock and where cargo could be unloaded and loaded, and Genoa for pleasure, a chance to visit friends.

The *William Black* remained at Leghorn for six weeks on this first voyage in 1824. The return journey brought her back to Liverpool by August 12th, a round trip of four months and seven days, after which master and crew were discharged and paid. They were all local men and could look forward to a spell on land.

Bureaucracy is not a modern invention, and John may well have cursed the Admiralty's clerks at times. In October 1826, on his return from Leghorn on a later voyage, John learned that the Admiralty had stopped his half-pay because he had been late in applying for its renewal. He explained by letter that his application had been delayed 'owing to an unusual long passage I experienced in the Mediterranean, which was prolonged by adverse winds fifty days beyond my expectation'.[3] Quite how John calculated his fifty-day delay is not ours to know, but this journey had indeed been unusually slow. He had sailed from Liverpool on December 28th, 1825, and had not arrived in Leghorn until February 13th. A journey that had taken just twenty-four days the previous summer now kept him at sea for forty-seven days. The Admiralty accepted his explanation as plausible. Despite the relentless progress of the Industrial Revolution, an unfavourable wind could delay a journey under sail to the Mediterranean by several weeks.

John Monk's second voyage on the *William Black* nearly ended in disaster before the brig had even left the Irish Sea. He was joined on board by a young passenger, who travelled with him from Liverpool, seizing the opportunity to get his first sight of the Mediterranean, although without anything so mundane as the right paperwork. John was 36 at this time, and the passenger seems to have been a younger gentleman. His guest kept a detailed diary of the journey, recording all of its various twists and turns.

The writer's choice of terminology suggests that he was a mariner who knew his way around a ship and her sails, but his seasickness suggests he was not recently at sea. The two men do not seem to have been close friends before the journey. It may be that the passenger had met John socially while in Liverpool. John seems to have invited him to join him, an offer that the passenger had accepted at the last minute. Frustratingly, the author's name on the front cover is indistinct and not quite legible.

The diary gives a sense of the unpredictable pace and nature of a voyage at sea on a Georgian sailing ship. The first and more interesting half covers the stormy and eventful journey from Liverpool to Leghorn and an enforced stay in quarantine on arrival. The master, crew and passenger travel through a violent storm and heavy seas which bring them close to disaster, and then wait for a breeze on a glassy, becalmed Mediterranean. There is a dramatic rescue, injury and even a death on board. The diary entries are repeated here near verbatim. The only changes are to improve readability where the writer uses short-hand notes and to edit down some of the longer geographical descriptions.

The *William Black* sailed from Liverpool on October 10th, 1827, just as a major storm was sweeping in from the Atlantic.

John's decision to depart with bad weather on the way, and at the beginning of the annual stormy period, may have been influenced by commercial pressures but may also be a sign of his relative inexperience as master at this point. The *William Black* was not alone in putting out to sea, though, as more than two hundred vessels were wrecked or driven ashore around the coast of the British Isles during the days of this particularly fierce storm.[4]

A stormy departure[5]

SUNDAY 10th October 1824 –

We sailed at one p.m. from the River Mersey, at 2 rounded the Black Rock, the wind East South-East with heavy rain, and at 4 the pilot left us. At 7 heavy gusts of wind accompanied with rain, the ship taking much water on deck. We hauled the trysail and pumped the ship dry out. At 8 strong gales with heavy squalls. Lowered the topsail on the cap.

At 8.30 a heavy sea struck the starboard quarter, which hove the ship on her larboard beam. The foretopsail, foresail and the fore-topmast tag sail all blew to pieces. We cut away the main topsail sheets. The ship was lying on her beam ends with the lower yardarms in the water for several minutes. The man at the helm was knocked down and was some minutes insensible. The main topgallant sail split and carried the yard away in the slings. About 8.45 she righted, having carried away all her larboard bulwarks and cleared the decks. The Master and crew got the ship before the wind and scudded upon bare poles.

Being in this precarious situation it was determined to turn for Holyhead, but it was found impossible owing to so great a sea being on. Therefore, the only chance left was to make for Dublin or scud before the wind down channel. The sea and wind still continued unabated and the Master, finding two of his men dangerously hurt, thought it most prudent to adopt the latter course. The weather continued very boisterous, thick and hazy with rain. We scudded down under bare poles for 48 hours when we got into the Bay of Biscay.

During the gale, I was in the cabin and heard the Master twice cry out that the vessel was going down and ordering the men to cut away the sails. The men at this time were so alarmed that not one of them would go aloft to do this and the Master actually went up himself, which caused the righting of the ship.

Our situation at this awful crisis may be conceived, I cannot however attempt to describe it. I remained during the whole night sitting on the side of my bed, having no person to converse with, except now and then when the cabin boy made his appearance and from whom I repeatedly enquired if all danger was now over. He, unconscious of that which had happened, very innocently and coolly replied 'Yes, it was only a storm!'

MONDAY. At 2 p.m. had a little biscuit and beef steak, having neither eat nor drank since breakfast the preceding day.

THURSDAY. Heavy gales from the westward with squalls and rain and hail. The Master furled all sails and hove to on the larboard tack under balanced reef'd trysail. At midnight, fresh breeze from the North-East. Wore ship and made sail.

SATURDAY. Strong gales from the Eastward with a heavy sea. At 2 p.m. we saw a brig with signals of distress flying and made sail towards her. At 3, lowered the topsails on the cap and ran close past the vessel, the captain of which informed us she was full of water and going down. Captain Monk, having resolved to save the lives of the crew, hove to, although the sea was running mountains high, upon which the captain of the other vessel made an attempt to run alongside of us. Had he been permitted to have done so, both vessels might have been lost and therefore Captain Monk hailed him to get into his boat with his crew and he would pick them up, it being the only means of saving their lives, which he did in a most seamanlike manner. Nor shall I soon forget the anxiety and activity displayed by the whole of our crew upon the occasion.

She proved to be the brig *Elizabeth* of Great Yarmouth, Benjamin Quinton master, bound for Lisbon having been at sea for ten days from Plymouth. Our humanity exceeded that of two other vessels that had run close by her without attempting to render them any relief although signals of distress had been flying for two days. The captain and his 5 men were made as comfortable as our vessel would allow.

Journeying south

SUNDAY. The weather proved more moderate and we made great way, at least seven knots the whole day.

MONDAY. Made the rock of Lisbon after breakfast. I arose, lopped my neck's beard and went upon deck. The views of the

Portugal coast were very fine. I remained on deck a considerable time, the climate at least 10 degrees warmer than in England.

WEDNESDAY. This day equally as pleasant as yesterday. I wrote a long letter to SP.[6] I related my sudden departure for Liverpool and the occurrences of the voyage etc thus far. To send with Captain Quinton, whom we hoped to lose together with his crew by putting them on board of a homeward bound vessel or on shore at Gibraltar in the course of tomorrow. Had a long *tête-à-tête* with the Master as to the Neston and Parkgate belles. Found out he had a sneaking notion of Miss Sally Russell, one of the finest girls in Staffordshire etc?? Missus Marshall would not go down even with 75,000. Oh, rare Oh! The vanity of one or the imperfections of the other must be excessive.[7]

THURSDAY. A beautiful day. Heat oppressive rather than comfortable, with little or no wind.

This conversation, while sailing off the coast of Portugal, is the first mention of Sally, perhaps John Monk's most significant romantic entanglement and the woman with whom he would come closest to marriage. Based on surviving correspondence with other members of her family, Sally was probably Sarah Russell, the eldest daughter of the industrialist James Russell of Bescot Hall, Walsall, a landowner and gas-tube manufacturer at Wednesbury Crown Tube Works.

John and Sally may have become acquainted three months earlier, on a warm summer evening in August 1824, when John, his brothers Charles and Joseph and a Miss Russell were all present on Parkgate parade for a society promenade, which was reported with the usual delight by the *Chester Courant*:

The parade, by the sea side, at Parkgate, on Sunday evening last, for a brilliant display of elegant females, exceeded everything of the kind we have witnessed for many years; the fineness of the weather, and the beauty of the scenery, brought down many respectable families from the adjacent country, and together with the regular visitors, which are numerous, formed a most interesting group, and rendered this charming place if possible more enchanting than ever.[8]

The manners and social function of the promenade at Parkgate would have been similar to Jane Austen's portrayals of London and Bath, albeit on a smaller, more provincial scale. Austen's first novel *Sense and Sensibility* had been published just thirteen years earlier, and her last novels *Northanger Abbey* and *Persuasion* were printed only five years before John and Sally took their summer stroll through Parkgate.

Promenading was a favourite pastime for the Georgian upper classes. Ladies and gentlemen would don their finest clothes and take a stroll in the late afternoon along the waterfront or through a city park. There were the benefits of fresh air and exercise, but these were also social occasions. Young men and women could share admiring glances as they strolled serenely by. Women could draw attention to themselves and excite passions amongst the men present with subtle flirtations, displays of femininity and fine clothes. In 1733, the author PQ wrote in *St James's Park: A Comedy* that promenading 'carries so much the appearance of Innocence, yet at the same time has all the opportunities of Vice'.[9]

John's conversation on the *William Black* had ended with

the discouraging revelation that Sarah's mother would not be persuaded of his suitability, even with a fortune of £75,000. The reference to Marshall instead of Russell is likely to be a slip of the pen. These may have been comments made jokingly after several glasses of wine in the master's cabin, but it appears that John had some work to do to convince Sally's parents that he was a good match for their daughter.

A few days later, after the two men talk again about the young women back in England, the writer will note that he suspects John is a 'General Lover'. The term had appeared in a novel of letters called *The General Lover, Or Small Talker* (1769),[10] a cautionary tale about rogues who charm their way into ladies' hearts only to cast them cruelly aside, and had more recently been used in a comic opera of 1803 to describe a military man with a tendency to chase women wherever he went. Either way, it suggests Sally's mother may have had good cause to be wary!

> *Oh, chide not, my charmer, nor think me a rover,*
> *A Soldier, of course, is a general lover;*
> *With a row dow, stand clear all,*
> *Ye beauties, both high and low;*
> *Oh, in love still I must fall,*
> *Sweet creatures, where'er I go.*[11]

SATURDAY. The morning was fine but the afternoon became cloudy and in the evening it became very squally with rain. During the night it rained the heaviest I ever heard, accompanied with lightning. Made no way.

SUNDAY. The middle of the day was very fine. The view of Cadiz and the country on the east side was very interesting, the latter very much like Mossley Hill and neighbourhood, interspersed with gentlemen's villas and country seats. Evening became boisterous and wet, the wind veering round the compass. There was an excellent haloing light off Cadiz on a tower 172 feet high, on the principle of the South Stack lighthouse, Holyhead.

MONDAY. The weather was wet, thick and hazy and nothing to be seen. I was therefore in the cabin the whole day. Captain now and then giving us an account of the victory obtained on the plains we were crossing by the gallant Nelson, 21 Oct 1805.

The Mediterranean

TUESDAY. The morning weather was very thick but cleared up about 11. The coast on each side was very rocky and mountainous in the afternoon. The views were beautiful and the towers on the different capes somewhat like summer houses on the hills in Westmoreland and Cumberland.

Tarifa is strongly fortified but for what I could not discern, the country being of the most barren nature and neither man or beast to be seen. There is here a high tower with a light thereon. The Spanish flag was hoisted and in compliment we hoisted our Union Jack as we passed.

The wind getting up and a strong current running with us, we soon got in sight of Gibraltar Rock, which is immensely large but contrasting it with that of Apex Hill[12] on the opposite coast of Africa was somewhat like comparing Buxton Castle to

145

the Meckin in Wales – it actually appeared as if in the clouds. The scenery around about 4 o'clock was truly grand, and there were 15 sail carrying all the canvass they could bear. Our ship however soon left several of them astern. Between 5 and 6 we prepared Captain Quinton and his crew to leave us and about 6 they were put on board the brig *Metamorphose*, Captain Hughs, becalmed in the Bay of Gibraltar, having expressed their thanks for the kindness they received on board our ship.

The sun setting and going down exceeded anything of the kind I ever witnessed before. The town and fortifications of Santa had a very good effect but that of Gibraltar, as far as we could see it, had little or nothing to praise.

THURSDAY. This was a most delightful day and the land could be seen a considerable distance. The mountains upon the island of Grenada are much higher than any of the preceding and, although the heat was as great as in the middle of summer in England, we could see snow upon the summit of the mountain. The day being so fine our dinner table was laid out upon deck, having a sail suspended over us for an awning. Two or three turtle made their appearance. At night spent two hours playing cribbage with Captain and got defeated. Made little way, being a dead calm.

FRIDAY. Warm but thick and misty. At 9 a.m. we passed close by a small island called Alboran, about ½ miles in extent and not more than 15 to 20 feet in height to appearance, whereon are large quantities of wild fowl. Numbers who have been in the habit of travelling the Mediterranean for years, never could discover it, although laid down in charts. At night a breeze sprung up and continued.

SATURDAY. At 8 a.m. we made Cape de Gaeta and during the day, which was in shore rather foggy, we had a pretty good view of the plains of Almeria where the illustrious hero Wellington and his army so successfully conquered the French in 1811. All along these stupendous rocks are small towers about a mile distant from each other, as if erected for the purpose of reconnoitring.

The breeze continued to favour us the whole of this day. Had a good laugh at the expense of ___ with the Captain, who I now begin to suspect is a General Lover. He spoke highly of the Misses Dallas of Manchester whom he met at a ball at Parkgate on 7th and 8th October, and intends calling upon them when he next trips to Manchester.

SUNDAY. Stiff breeze with a heavy sea which caused the ship to pitch a good deal. I became sick and remained so during the day, consequently was little on deck. The sun shone brilliantly.

The nausea and vomiting suffered by the diary writer would be familiar to most seamen at one time or another. Many experienced mariners suffer seasickness, perhaps the most famous being Admiral Nelson. Writing from HMS *Victory* in 1804, he confided in a letter that he still struggled with it after thirty years at sea: 'I am ill every time it blows hard and nothing but my enthusiastic love for my profession keeps me one hour at sea'.[13]

The Bay of Biscay, through which John and his guest sailed as the storm in the North Atlantic abated, is infamous among mariners. Atlantic waves tend to be long and high because of the great distance across the ocean and the extreme depth of water. The curve of the Biscay coastline gathers these rollers and bounces them back into a comparatively small area, creating large waves and confused waters.

By contrast, sailors in the Mediterranean face a different set of conditions. The tidal range may be small, but winds can whip up short, sharp waves which can be equally unsettling to the stomach, as the diary writer was now discovering.

When Napoleon Bonaparte created a camel corps during his 1798 campaign in Egypt, the distinctive loping gait of the animal, known as 'ships of the desert', left many of his men seasick and unable to fight. The corps had initially been comprised of infantrymen, but Bonaparte soon replaced them with marines, reasoning that they were more accustomed to the motion at sea.[14]

MONDAY. I took a dose of the Captain's salts which removed the ill effects of yesterday. On deck all day and was much gratified, the day being fine. We had a fine view of the mountain from off Alicant up the coast including Benedorme to Cape Antonio and gladly would have paid an artist according to the strength of my purse for a sketch of them. The sunset was sublime and surpassed all the skies I ever before witnessed, indeed enough to make one doubt its being the 1st November.

I am fully convinced that the Italian scenery I had frequently seen displayed upon canvas was not at all exaggerated, particularly looking back to the rocks called St Paul, which had the appearance of being on the surface of the water. Never was mahogany more variegated. The wind being favourable we had a good run both yesterday and today.

The Benedorme Mountain, of which I took the best sketch I could, is that in which the Carthaginians under Hannibal cut an entrenchment, not being able in any other manner to penetrate them so as to convey their baggage etc. This mountain with the gap is to be seen at a considerable distance and serves as a guide to mariners, by whom it is called Cuchillada de Roldan or St George's Gap.

TUESDAY. This was a day equally as serene as yesterday without any wind, we were off Cape Antonio until evening.

WEDNESDAY. We were out of sight of land but the wind was very scanty. About midday we were in a strong current which could not be accounted for. At 6 p.m. we interred the poor black cook who was released from his miseries about 2 a.m. this morning, the Captain performing a very short service. I never wish to witness a funeral at sea again.

FRIDAY. Rather more mild with the appearance of a stormy evening. Large burr or halo being observed round the moon. Played cribbage with Captain until ½ past 10, got worst'd 2 games. The wind got up and the captain depressed my spirits by saying we must expect a storm as we were approaching the Gulf of Lyons, which he had never crossed without experiencing a storm. Indeed he stated that, during his being off Toulon in 1811-14 with the British fleet under Lord Exmouth watching for the French, it blew a gale for 11 months and 3 weeks, during which time several vessels sank.

SATURDAY. At 4 a.m. the Captain's Watch announced that it blew hard. Captain and mate up. The confusion, noises and bustle on deck were indescribable, cries of haul that sail, reef etc. Completely alarmed me. At 5 when Captain turned in, I enquired as to the cause of noises on deck 'only a North Wester in the Gulf of Lyons as I had you expect'.

The sea roll'd on deck and struck the vessel like great guns. All the shutters, doors etc were closed. The gale increased and continued till 8 p.m.. I was so completely floor'd that I could not get up. The vessel rolled in all directions. One sea struck and filled the fore topsails, carried the longboat out of the chocks and started the roundhouse, and the Captain expected the foremast was carried away, the weight of water must have been 20 tons.

At 10 p.m. the storm ceased and the wind veered round to the east, direct against us. Within the last 24 hours we have run 160 miles. To dinner today, indeed had I been inclined, I must have been disappointed, the caboose (the ship's stove in a small deckhouse) being useless.

TUESDAY. Beating up to a sad tune. Not making 20 miles. We passed Frejus where Bonaparte embarked for Elba. This evening rather clear, I saw Cape Garoupe where he landed on his return from Elba in 1815. Weather very cold.

WEDNESDAY. Rather warmer but little wind. In the evening a fine breeze which lasted a few hours, improved my hopes of getting to Leghorn tomorrow.

THURSDAY. I went on deck at sunrise and had a fine view of the island of Corsica, very high, which we passed in the course of the day. 'Hopes blighted'. No wind, no Leghorn this evening. Could see little of the Alps, except snow on the summit, being at least 100 miles off. The day was very warm.

FRIDAY. There was little wind and that from the East was direct against us, beating off a small island about 2 miles in length, Gorgona, with little advantage. The Pyrenees mountains had a pretty effect. Although not near so high as the high land of Corsica, they bear a great resemblance. At 9 p.m. a light breeze sprung up from S W, continued till 12 when it became a dead calm & so continued all night, indeed we might have gone to Gorgona for anchovies.

Arrival at Leghorn

SATURDAY. At 8 a.m. Leghorn was in sight. I arose and ate a hearty breakfast, hoping it might be last on board ship. The jolly boat was hauled out, manned etc, and the ship towed in for at least 4 miles – it being dangerous going in, in consequence of a large bank called Malora Bank running out to a considerable distance and we had only from seven to eight fathoms of water. Leghorn lies upon a plain, having the Pyrenees mountains close to the north east, and in the perspective with high land on the south much resembling Bagillt from Parkgate. It appears to be about the size of Chester but deficient of those majestic towers for which that ancient city is so much admired. The entrance into the harbour, miserable houses built of brick and plastered.

When near the harbour the quarantine boat came aft, hailed us and, our answers being satisfactory, assisted (of course for a handsome donation) in towing us in. When we arrived at the mole at ¼ past 4, all hands mustered on deck but, as I had no pass, was passed off as one of the men and obliged to shew myself, upon which occasion I unfortunately blushed!

At 5 Captain went on shore to the Product Office but returned with 2 officers who remained with us all night, not being able to accomplish his object but quite sanguine of succeeding in the morning. My packing up and preparing for disembarking proved rather premature and my disappointment was great but hopes of doing so in the morning buoyed up my spirits.

Quarantine measures in the early nineteenth century were widely resented by merchants. They were often inconsistent between ports, were open to corruption and could cause lengthy and expensive delays. The real problem, though, was that the issue that quarantine was attempting to solve was so poorly understood. Outbreaks of plague, cholera and yellow fever regularly killed thousands, but medical opinion at the time was still divided as to how such diseases were spread. Battle lines were drawn between contagionists, who believed diseases could be spread from person to person, and miasmatists, who held the more traditional view that disease was the result of an impure atmosphere, where an unsanitary environment like a slum could create a noxious miasma, which hung in the air.

Later in the century, pioneering scientists would finally silence the miasma theory in favour of germ theory. Among them were John Snow, who mapped outbreaks of cholera in London in 1854 and traced the source to a Broadstreet water pump built just three feet from a cesspit, and Louis Pasteur, who did more formal experiments in the 1860s into the relationship between germ and disease.

All this was at least thirty years away, though, for John and his passenger in 1824. The system they encountered in Leghorn was the subject of widespread complaint and ridicule. At the same time that the men of the *William Black* were undergoing their quarantine of observation, an article appeared in the *Bath Chronicle and Weekly Gazette*, which shows how Italian quarantine procedures were viewed and recounts a wonderful anecdote, real or apocryphal:

The quarantine regulations in the Italian and especially in the Neapolitan states are proverbially ridiculous as well as vexatious... A vessel released from quarantine at Leghorn was again put under it for nineteen days, in consequence of a monkey belonging to the captain, having jumped from his vessel to another which had not performed quarantine, and back again to his vessel.[15]

SUNDAY morning. I awoke to the ringing of bells, sounds of music, cries of the petit traders etc all round us. Arose and went upon deck and under our stern a band of musicians was playing Yankee Doodle. This, upon enquiry, I found was the practice every Sunday morning, being what the musicians termed serenading, for which they rely upon the liberality of the captains and crews of vessels. There were numerous traders with their various commodities displayed in their boats for sale, principally Jews. Captain went to the Product Office but hope was deferred again until tomorrow. Mr Peel,

Mr Hamilton etc came along side of us. Sent for my letters, the farce most ludicrous.

MONDAY. It has been determined that we should remain 10 days in quarantine. Hopes blighted. Wrote S.N.H.,[16] detailing our voyage and our abominable treatment here, requesting him to use his wonted exertions in making it public.

TUESDAY. I resolved upon addressing the consul, conceiving it would do no harm and might do good, to which the Captain assented and to which he received the following -

British Consulate, Leghorn 18th Nov 1824

Sir

I beg to acknowledge the receipt of your letter of the 16th inst., informing me you have been placed under quarantine, in consequence of having saved and taken on board your vessel, the crew of the Brig Elizabeth of Yarmouth.

I have represented to the Board of Health how your very meritorious conduct on this occasion in the hope that every possible indulgence might be afforded you, and although they seem sensible of your deserts, they are, nevertheless, obliged to enjoin the rules presented on all similar occasions via the performance of ten days quarantine.

Should you be of the opinion that your cargo is likely to suffer from the quarantine permission will be granted you immediately to send whatever part of it you may think proper in the lazaretto.

Sincerely sir, your very obliged humble –

John Falconar, Consul

WEDNESDAY. I wrote to Miss ___ detailing the particulars of my recent misfortunes, pleasures etc. Mr Woolley from Messrs Peel and Ewbanks visited us and brought us Paris papers from 25 Oct to 1 inst. These tended greatly to assist in driving dark cares away.

THURSDAY. Received Paris papers from 16 Oct to 24th in which I observed some short accounts of the storm, and how great its ravages had been at Dublin, whence we were desirous of making but fortunately could not.

FRIDAY, SATURDAY, SUNDAY. During these days, several gents came alongside of us pitying our misfortunes. Made a purchase of a violin for 12 ½ paols.

MONDAY. In poor spirits, it having been stated I could not disembark having no pass. Captain Monk devising several ways for me to elude the interference of the Grand Duke and his harpies in office. I resolved not to play any *mise de garde* but apply instantly to the British Consul and if necessary to write by first post to London for the needful.

TUESDAY. I arose at ¼ past 7. At 8 the Doctor came alongside and all hands were arraigned like so many felons to be gazed at by he and 12 others in his state barge. Counting over the notes in the Bill of Health, he merely asked one of the guardianos if all were well and, he answering *Tooti Tooti*, he politely bowed and moved off, upon which a band of 8 fiddlers struck up a lively air by way of congratulating us upon our release from imprisonment.

The guardianos dows'd their belts, received ½ a dollar to drink our healths, and left us. Thus ended the farce of our illegal imprisonment of 10 days called a Quarantine of Observation!! Not a question put to one of us, much less strictly examined our pulsation.

Breakfast over, I made ready for disembarkation, anxiously looked out for the waterman to take us ashore. At eleven Mr Peel arrived, with whom Captain Monk and I went to Leghorn. Although its first approach presented greater misery than I had ever before witnessed, never was I more elated at approaching *terra firma*, upon which I stepped with more alacrity than I have for some time been wont.

Finally free to disembark, John Monk, his crew, and the unnamed passenger spent several weeks in Leghorn, while cargo was unloaded and the brig was made ready for departure. For John, the time ashore was a mix of work and pleasure. He spent time with local agents Peel and Woolley, but also made time for sightseeing, good food and relaxation, and acted as a tour guide for his guest.

The diarist's visit to Leghorn came nine years after the end of the long war but the English-speaking community was already strong in Leghorn, to the point where the only things missing from the visitor's account of his time in Italy are any Italians.

He received offers of assistance from the Vice-Consul, Mr Maddock, who hailed from Chester, and befriended 'Mr Deacon, a Sheffield gent' before being introduced to a surgeon from Liverpool. His evenings were spent playing bridge with expatriate merchants and other acquaintances of John, and, when the weather was wet, days were spent reading copies of

English newspapers. Dinners were sociable affairs, and English-speaking dining companions were plentiful:

Dined with Captain Monk... at the Table d'Hote, which consisted of soup, stewed fish, lamb etc... dessert consisting of grapes, apples, pears, almonds, raisins etc and was much pleased with the company, of whom only 8 in number were English, Irish, Welsh and Scotch!!

The highlight of the stay came one Sunday, when John, his guest, and three others took a coach to Pisa, fifteen miles away. The journey was comfortable, and they were able to admire the fine views of the Apennines on the left and the Mount Nero Hills on the right. They found Pisa to be an attractive, small town of just ten thousand people, with no notable commerce or manufacturing, but commented that it was busy with visitors, drawn by the mild winter climate. They marvelled at the profusion of fine buildings, particularly the Duomo, the Campo Santo and of course the Campanile, or leaning tower.

Like every tourist throughout the centuries, they discussed the possible reasons for the tower's lean. Climbing to the top, they admired the views towards Lucca and Florence, although the odd experience of walking up the slanting staircase made each of them feel as though they were falling.

After an overpriced dinner, they hurried down towards the River Arno, where they found Pisa's quayside thronged with people out walking. The writer considered it reminiscent of Hyde Park, although apparently without the same beauty or elegance. They were just in time to board the coach back to Leghorn.

The weather turned bad during the next week, and the writer spent most of his time inside, not often venturing out, except for

Sunday when he attended mass and made a tour of Leghorn's old English cemetery. The next day it was time to leave the city, as the *William Black* was ready to sail, and the diary ends.

In 1825, on John's return home from his next voyage, he would have learned about the alarming experience his cousin Richard had endured in March that year while attempting to return to India with his regiment.

The *Kent* was a ship of the East India Company, sailing with 641 people on board, including crew. Most of the passengers, like Richard, were soldiers of his regiment, many with their wives and children. The *Kent* had barely begun her long voyage to Bengal and China when she hit bad weather in the Bay of Biscay. She had battled through storms for two days when a fire broke out in the hold. The master tried to partially flood the ship to extinguish the growing flames but without success.

The *Kent*'s distress signal was spotted by the small brigantine *Cambria*, bound for Mexico with a crew of just eleven and about twenty Cornish miners, who decided to use the brigantine's boats to attempt a rescue. The raging storm was not the only danger they faced. As the fire spread through the burning ship, it would only be a matter of time before the first flame reached the gunpowder in the ship's magazine. Despite the increasing danger, the sailors and miners continued to make trip after trip back to the *Kent* as they ferried hundreds of survivors to the tiny *Cambria*.

The *Kent*'s magazine exploded early the following morning, by which time the *Cambria* was heavily loaded with more than 550 survivors, cramped and crowded on deck and in the cabin. The brigantine set sail for England, sitting worryingly low in the water. They were blessed with favourable winds, however, and arrived safely in Falmouth three days later. Richard was fortunate enough to be among the survivors, but eighty-one lives were lost.[17]

The story of the *Kent*'s destruction in 1825 would have been a reminder to John of familiar dangers. He had seen for himself within the last year the damage an Atlantic storm could do, and he would have known from his days on a man-of-war the risk posed by fire on a wooden ship. Although he now commanded a small merchant brig in a time of peace, and no longer faced French shore batteries or Danish gunboats in a ship of the line, the risks he faced in the merchant service were surprisingly similar. Less than ten percent of deaths at sea in the Royal Navy were the result of enemy action. The rest were due to accident, weather or disease, all risks faced equally by the merchant service. The death rate in merchant shipping was among the highest of any occupation.

Even when winds were good and seas were calm, a life in command could be lonely and stressful, as Macnamara and Brace would have found during their naval careers. John had responsibility for discipline, the health of his crew, and the condition of the vessel, as well as all the worries about the safe delivery of his cargo and making a profit. The weather meant the fate of a voyage would sometimes be out of his hands, but every delay would hit the overall profitability.

Another near disaster came in the winter of 1827, as John Monk was bringing the *William Black* home from Leghorn to Liverpool with a cargo of Indian corn. The events that followed were reported in some detail by the *Chester Courant* on February 13th, although the latitude reported was incorrect.

John and his crew had left Leghorn late in December and had probably reached the Atlantic before the weather started to deteriorate. The cold January wind grew stronger and reached gale force, blowing hard from the north, and the sea grew extremely rough. John had the ship sailing under double-reefed main trysail, reducing the surface area of the sails to maintain a course through the storm without risking the mast being snapped by the fierce gusts.

The ship rolled, pitched and yawed dangerously, as John and the crew fought to keep control. When John later came to sell the *William Black* in 1828, he observed in the advert that the ship was 'Well adapted for a coasting vessel, as she carries a very large Cargo, at an easy draft of water'.[18] This shallow draft would have allowed greater manoeuvrability inshore during calm weather, but during storms such as that in the Irish Sea of 1824, or here in the Atlantic in 1827, the reduced stability would have worked against her.

The strength of the wind increased further, and one particularly powerful wave swamped the vessel. The combined force of the wave and wind tipped the brig onto her side, leaving her 'upon her beam ends' and at serious risk of capsizing. Everything on the decks, the bulwarks, boats and galley stove, was swept away. The storm continued for several hours, and the crew knew that, unless they could right her, their ship could be sunk by another large wave, sending each of them to their deaths. To catch the wind, John ordered the crew to attach their hammocks to the fore-rigging as makeshift sails. Finally, as a result of their efforts, they were able to right the vessel, bring her under control and get her running safely with a following wind.

They were safe from the immediate danger of the pounding waves, but their problems were far from over. The drinking water was ruined, and their food was saturated with saltwater. Worse still, the brig's hull had been damaged in the storm and the timbers were leaking badly. The crew took shifts to man the pumps round the clock. Ships' pumps at this time were basic chain affairs, a series of scoops carrying the water upwards as a handle was cranked. They were inefficient and physically exhausting to operate. On top of this, John and his crew of seven still had to sail the ship.

After five relentless days and nights, apparently with nothing to drink but spirits, they finally limped into Lisbon harbour, where they were placed under quarantine and given medical help. All were at the point of exhaustion, although fortunately with no worse injury than 'dreadful swellings in their hands and feet',[19] and perhaps rather sore heads.

With the time needed for recovery and repairs to their vessel, it would be a further three months before John and the men of the *William Black* arrived back in Liverpool in early April 1828.

Supplying the nation

The life of a merchant master meant that John Monk would spend large parts of the year at sea or in a distant Mediterranean port. When absent from Liverpool, his business interests were in the hands of his agent, George Yates. Yates advertised the expected departure dates and destinations for each of the vessels on his roster and took orders in advance from Liverpool businesses and merchants, to ensure that each had a cargo ready to load. Agents in Leghorn and Dublin took similar roles. Liverpool's newspapers published arrival and departure dates under the title Shipping Intelligence, occasionally adding a few words on what an arriving vessel was carrying. The cargo with which John returned varied from one voyage to the next, but regularly included baled goods or barrels of alcohol. Sometimes, though, the contents of the hold were more unusual.

Sometimes the *William Black*'s cargo was comprised of multiple smaller items which would not be out of place in the back of a modern-day removal van. In November 1827, John arrived with a varied load, listed in detail by *Gore's Liverpool General Advertiser*. Among the cargo of up to 115 tons were pictures, objects of fine art, marble and cut stone, a table, alabaster vases, artificial flowers and silk, as well as wine, opium, casks of cream tartar, a barrel of anchovies and a Parmesan cheese.[20]

It is quite common to find this kind of art and statuary among the cargo list as John returned to England from the Mediterranean. During the eighteenth and nineteenth centuries, the Grand Tour of Europe became an educational and social rite of passage for the nobility's offspring. Wealthy young men and some women would make an extended voyage through northern Mediterranean countries, exploring classical antiquity and the art and architecture of the Renaissance. Italy was a particularly important part of the tour, with visits to Rome, Venice and Naples on every traveller's itinerary, and Leghorn was often the point of arrival or departure. As they explored Europe, travellers purchased souvenirs, often copies of Renaissance paintings or replicas of classical sculptures. Each of these had to be carefully packaged and delivered, ready for the buyer to find on their return to England.

In 1833, having sold the *William Black* and now master of the *Monk*, John made a rare foray further south down the Italian coast, docking first at Naples and then at Palermo, Sicily. Shortly before his departure, he wrote to Richard Grosvenor, expressing his pleasure at learning of his friend's 'complete restoration to health':

I am at the point of sailing for Naples and Palermo from one of which ports I will procure a case of choice liqueurs & in the mean time beg your Lordship's acceptance of two solitary bottles of Maraskins which have been on board the Monk some time.[21]

Twenty years earlier, during the war with Napoleon's brother-in-law, the King of Naples, John had been with the British fleet which had moored in the Bay of Naples and threatened to bombard the city. His return as a merchant master in 1833 came during one of his shorter voyages, taking just three months and twelve days, although without the usual visit to Dublin on the return leg. The *Liverpool Mercury* announced the *Monk*'s return on August 30th, and helpfully itemised what she carried:

1 hogshead wine, TA Browne and Co.. 4 pipes 15 hogshead 30 quarter cask ditto, Rathbone Brothers and Co.. 48 tons brimstone, 12 tons pumice stone, Ross Brothers... 1 quarter cask wine, 1 case cordials, J Monk... 5 pipes, 19 hogshead, 10 quarter cask wine, 20 pipes brandy, 16 cask cream tartar, 246 bags linseed, 1200 bags shumac, order -- Q Dk.[22]

The largest part of the cargo with which John returned to Liverpool was brimstone, literally 'burning stone', the contemporary name for sulphur. Until the end of the nineteenth century, most of the world's supply came from large deposits in Sicily, from where John was returning with forty-eight tons in the hold. The distinctive yellow powder and crystals were used to make gunpowder, matches and other products, and could be converted to sulphuric acid. As Britain industrialised, demand for brimstone was booming.

Brimstone matches and tinderboxes were used through the Georgian era until friction matches entered general use in the 1830s. Each match was a wooden splint, dipped in brimstone at either end. A flint and steel was used to send a spark into a tin of flammable fabric, the tinder box, from which the match could be lit. The box could then be closed, and the sparks extinguished.

Brimstone match sellers were a common sight on English city streets, often older military men with no pension on which to rely. As Henry Mayhew recalled in 1851,

The brimstone match-sellers were of all ages, but principally... old people. Many of them... wore tattered regimentals, or some remains of military paraphernalia, and had been... soldiers, but not entitled to a pension; the same with seamen.[23]

Among the deliveries for merchants on this voyage to Sicily in 1833 were also personal orders. The cargo list includes '1 case cordials, J Monk', as John remembered his promise to Richard Grosvenor of a case of choice liqueurs. On a previous voyage to Gibraltar, he had returned with some African seeds as a gift for Lady Grosvenor, and on another he brought her a small handbag or reticule, wisely keeping on good terms with the wives of influential friends.

The ideal for any merchant master in John's position would be to have a number of long-lasting and dependable business relationships. To build and maintain such a network would have taken considerable time and effort, but after ten years as a merchant master on the *William Black* and the *Monk*, an advertisement in a Dublin paper in 1834 shows how it could benefit both parties. The proprietor of Del Vecchio advertised his new stock and assured his customers that he would have a regular supply of Italian produce in future:

Del Vecchio informs the trade that he has received, per the Monk, *Captain Monk, last from Leghorn, a few bales of Tuscan hemp, Lucca oil in jars, macaroni, vermicelli de genoa, parmesan cheese, Leghorn hats, &c &c. All of which he will dispose of wholesale, on moderate terms. Del Vecchio will be regularly supplied with the above, and many other articles of Italian produce. 26 Westmoreland-street, Dec 9, 1834.*

Britons in the Georgian era were increasingly familiar with pasta, such as the macaroni and vermicelli with which John had returned, as young travellers returned from their Grand Tours with a taste for it. To Georgian ears, though, a 'macaroni' was also slang for a young man who had returned home from Europe with affected or ostentatious Continental manners. Pasta grew slowly in popularity in Britain through the Victorian era, but it was not until the twentieth century that it became a true staple with the general public.

As well as the gifts of liqueurs and cigars for friends and family, John occasionally brought back items for himself. When he docked at Bristol in 1830, at the end of his maiden voyage on the *Monk*, listed alongside the commercial cargo of wheat and one hundred barrels of anchovies is 'J. Monk, 3 cases alabaster'. Similar boxes of alabaster appear among the cargo on other voyages as, over the years, John built a collection of classical alabaster statues.

During the visit to Leghorn in November 1824, documented by the unnamed passenger, John took the author to Giacinto Micali's Emporium,[24] a well-known seller of reproduction antiquities, where they admired the classical paintings and replica statuary. They perused them longingly, before deciding that the prices were beyond their budgets:

FRIDAY. With Captain Monk through Micali's Repository of Statuary etc of a very great extent. The alabaster most beautiful and with which I was much taken, particularly with the Rape of the Sabines, after that at Florence by Ino. Of Bologna and for which with cover, call etc 60 dollars was asked. Found in my heart to offer 40! There were from 40 to 50 fine paintings, originals and the most celebrated artists, the price of which however exceeded the limits of either our purses, although we greatly wished to possess one or two of them.[25]

John may have seen these alabaster figures as a practical investment in high-quality, collectable items, but their emotional significance would have run deeper. He had been serving in the Royal Navy when many young men of status were doing their Grand Tours and he was certainly no 'macaroni'. Letters show his manner on occasion to be blunt and direct, particularly when angered, and he would be described in later years by a judge and acquaintance as 'a man of simple habits'.[26] He spent much of his adult life at sea, in berths or cabins with rudimentary facilities, and often with only the conversation of his crewmates for company. The delicate lines of the carved alabaster may have helped quell any lingering doubts John had about his own sophistication and good taste, as he sought to associate with the upper echelons of Cheshire society.

It is perhaps telling that, fifty years later, when John sat down to write his will, alongside the charitable donations and the general division of his wealth and land, the only personal possession he mentioned individually was his collection of alabaster statues:

5. I bequeath all my alabaster figures to my said nephew William Monk Gibbon.[27]

On those occasions when John returned to Liverpool with baled goods such as cotton or silk, he is likely to have had direct dealings with his brothers Charles and Joseph in their roles with the customs service. John's brig was one of thousands of merchant vessels that converged on Liverpool each year from all corners of the world and, at a time of basic medicinal understanding and no antibiotics, the fear of the plague, cholera and other contagious diseases was ever-present. Liverpool's two floating lazarettos were purely for the reception of clean-bill ships, arriving from countries with no recent reports of plague. Nonetheless, certain types of cargo, such as cotton, wool or silk, were deemed to need airing for either fifteen or forty days, closely guarded throughout by the two Monk brothers.[28]

John Monk commanded the *William Black* for five years, from 1824 to 1828, making eight trips between Liverpool, Dublin and Leghorn. His association with the brig ended in December 1828, when he arrived back in Dublin from a journey to

Leghorn and listed her for sale. John had been the majority shareholder since 1826, after which Lloyds Register listed the ownership as 'Captain & Co'.[29] Following his brush with disaster in the winter of 1827, when he and his crew had nearly met their deaths off the Portuguese coast, John may have felt that it was no longer wise to be travelling the Atlantic in what he considered a shallow-draft coasting vessel. Family connections were useful again and John directed enquiries either to himself as master on board or to one of his brothers-in-law, Edward Acton Gibbon at the Dublin Ballast Office, or John Brown, the auctioneer in Chester.[30]

Records show the *William Black* was initially bought back by her original owner and was then sold on to a Mr Croker. The final record came in 1833, when the brig went missing on her way back from Portugal. There is no mention of her in the following year's *Lloyd's Register*, suggesting the *William Black*, in which John had himself had come close to disaster on several occasions, was most likely either sunk or wrecked.[31]

7. The *Monk*

It would be another eighteen months before John would next command a merchant vessel, making 1829 a rare year spent on land. The year began on a sad note, however, with the death of his mother Esther on January 30th, at the age of 70. The children had been concerned about her declining health for several years already, as shown by a letter from Joseph to Nessie back in 1826:

She often complains. She now lays in bed until my father is up and dressed, and it does not hurry her so much. I have thought once or twice we should have lost her this summer, and when poorly she does not take care of herself for she must be always passing backwards and forwards in the kitchen, and something strikes me, we shall lose her first.[1]

Joseph was right to predict that their mother would be the first to go, but their father William would not be far behind. Joseph had fewer concerns about his father's wellbeing but was more bothered by his increasingly grumpy temperament, *'Father looks as well as ever I saw him. He eats hearty. I would as well if he would not be so cross'.* William died in September 1831, aged 78. His will was as short as could be and left everything to his eldest son, Charles.[2]

William's twin, Benjamin, for many years also neighbour and colleague at the Parkgate custom house, had died in Chester just a month earlier. Benjamin's final years had been marked by sadness, as he had mourned the loss of his son, Captain

Richard Monk, who had met a violent death in 1826. He had survived the Battle of Waterloo and the wrecking of the *Kent* in 1825, but Richard's luck ran out barely a year later, not long after he had returned to the East Indies.

The distance, bureaucracy and the slow speed at which news travelled meant that it would be the following June before a letter from the War Office confirmed the details of Richard's death to his brother Edward. His party had been in a boat on the Ganges on their way to Meerut. They were between Mezzapore and Allanabad and had moored for the night on a remote sand bank when they were set upon by robbers. Most of those on board were overpowered, bound with cord and left otherwise unharmed, but several later reported hearing a struggle in the dark, followed by the sound of something heavy been thrown overboard. After the attack, Richard could not be found, but his trunk had been forced open and his cabin ransacked. He was presumed drowned, although a corpse found nearby could not be positively identified.[3]

Richard was 41 when he died, unmarried and childless. He had been away for most of his adult life and had perhaps died too young for his nieces and nephews to know him as they would grow to know John. He was not forgotten, however, and many years later, a framed map hung in his nephew Charles Brown's office in Chester, marked decades earlier by Richard to show his route through Europe during the long fight with the French.[4]

This extended period on land in 1829 allowed John to enjoy the Chester and Liverpool social scene once more. The afternoon of Wednesday, May 6th, was spent at Chester racecourse. The May

Festival had been introduced in 1766 and was a firm highlight in the social calendar of the north-west of England. The first grandstand had been built just a decade earlier to accommodate the growing crowds. All of Georgian society spent the afternoon at the races, gambling, shouting and cheering as one. In the evening, working-class revellers would gather in the local pubs and inns, while the gentry headed to parties and balls. Following their afternoon at the racecourse, John and three hundred other guests attended a Grand Race Ball at the Albion Hotel.[5] This was more than a brief gathering. Guests arrived at ten o'clock, the dancing started an hour later and the party continued through until dawn, in a ballroom that was brightly lit and decorated with evergreens and flowers.

One Friday night in September, John Monk and Richard Grosvenor were among over seven hundred guests at a Grand Fancy Dress Ball at the Royal Hotel, Chester. It was a huge affair and was covered in detail by the *Chester Courant*, which included a near-exhaustive list of attendees and their outfits. The interior of the Royal Hotel on Eastgate Street had been converted into a faux stone hall for the occasion, in which tables groaned 'beneath a burthen of viands, the produce of almost every clime'. The doors were opened, and an orchestra played as guests flooded in. The reporter for the *Courant* went into overdrive with his praise. The ballroom was,

instantly filled with such a galaxy of lovely females as were never congregated before under the canopy of Heaven. Dressed sumptuously, yet with such propriety and modesty of taste, that their fascinating charms became a thousand times more bewitching.[6]

The costumes were often elaborate and heavily ornamented; some were tailor-made for the occasion, often on the theme of historical royalty or picturesque paupers. Queen Elizabeth, Louis XIV and Mary, Queen of Scots mingled happily with Swiss peasants, Robin Hood and Cinderella. Perhaps disappointingly, John chose to wear his formal Navy uniform, as was common for military officers.

Whether any of the 'galaxy of lovely females' at the ball in Chester caught John's eye is not recorded, but he was still an eligible bachelor. His expected marriage to Sally Russell had not come to pass. The signs had been promising. Two years after the promenade on Parkgate waterfront, the couple had still been considered to be close to marriage, and John's brother Joseph wrote, with his usual wit, to their sister Nessie in November 1826 that the family were expecting John and Sally to marry when he returned from his current voyage:

Next is the Captain. I believe he is going to be married to Miss Russell when he returns. If he doesn't marry better than his other brother he had better go through the steeple door and get one of the bell ropes to tie him instead of the parson.[7]

For whatever reason, though, the expected nuptials had not happened, and Sally Russell, whom John had adoringly referred to as 'the finest girl in Staffordshire', would later marry Reverend Francis Foreman Clarke in 1833. For all the respect that naval officers commanded, maybe they did not always make good husbands. As a merchant master, John was likely to be away for at least six months each year, in cities far away, doing she knew not what. In contrast, the Clarke family were regular visitors at the Russell home, and Sally may simply have decided that she needed a husband who would be more frequently present.

John and the Russell family seem to have remained close despite this. It is possible that everyone could relax, now that he was no longer seen as a suitor to their daughter. In a lively letter several years later, Sarah's youngest sister, Emma de Blois, treats John as a kindly uncle. She thanks him for the gift of a dress and teases him about his still being a sprightly young bachelor. John has seemingly joked to Emma that her father should build him a house for his retirement, to which she reports back playfully that her father has offered him a derelict worker's cottage on their estate.[8]

John was never to marry but, on occasion, letters portray him as a slightly roguish charmer. The diarist on the voyage to Leghorn had concluded that the Captain was a 'General Lover', and Emma de Blois Russell seemed to concur, enjoying her role as go-between in another of John's flirtations:

I told Miss Clarke the pretty things you said of her and she in return begs her very kind remembrance. I don't know whether she did not send a warmer message but it would not be discreet of me to deliver it.[9]

John seems to have known the power of a well-chosen gift, particularly for the women in his life. Men routinely get bottles of liqueurs, but John was confident enough to choose dresses and handbags for the women he knew. Exotic seeds also seemed to be a popular choice, and well received. Just as Emma was delighted with her new dress, John had also charmed his way into her mother's good books:

Mother begs to thank you for your kind offer and says she shall be much obliged for any Dahlia roots you can procure. The New Zealand and New South Wales seeds she is very much obliged to you for, and desires me to say she hopes to see you very soon again.

The summer of 1829 was spent as part of the organising committee for that year's Parkgate Regatta. As sons of the Parkgate customs officer and each with a maritime background, it was no surprise that brothers John and Charles became involved in the event. The village's first regatta had been held two years earlier, in 1827, after John Lloyd, already an organiser of the Chester Regatta and a regular visitor to Parkgate, had seen potential in its attractive promenade and wide expanse of water. The day had been fine and the event well attended. The regatta in 1828 was also a success, and the hope was that it would remain an annual event.

The summer of 1829, though, was a grim one. The weather had been terrible in the preceding months, a disaster for the local economy. Fishermen had lost boats in the storms, and many of the usual fashionable visitors to the village had stayed away. The regatta had been postponed for two weeks already, due to the continuing bad weather. Fortunately, conditions cleared sufficiently, and the committee prepared to go ahead on Thursday, September 17th, the event later being covered extensively in the *Chester Chronicle*.[10]

In an attempt to bring colour to a rainy day, John decorated his barge with naval flags, streaming from every point of her masts and rigging, and moored her opposite the hotel to mark the Start and Finish point for races. A small orchestra played for the assembled rain-soaked crowd. Four sailing and rowing races were planned for the day, with separate events for local fishermen and gentlemen amateurs. Four boats took part in the afternoon's first sailing race. *Mary* held the lead initially, then ran aground on a bank of silt and had to be refloated. The wind then died down almost completely, and progress was slow, but *Mary* eventually crossed the finish line in front. Next was a rowing race, using some of the same boats but with masts and sails removed. After that, the weather got worse, further racing was impossible and the event was finally postponed to the following day.

When competitors and organisers gathered again the next day, there was a new problem. Already contending with bad weather, poor attendance and the need to avoid sand banks, the organisers found that a disagreement had broken out between the boatsmen of the first race, with demands that it be rerun. The organisers conceded and at the second running the race was won by *Good Intent*, with the original winner, *Mary*, trailing in last. The big race of the day was between the first-class sailing boats. *Siren* led from *Ariel* before both made mistakes, and in the closing stretches *Maria* came through to win.

The *Advertiser* commented that, in the Royal Navy, the skippers of both *Siren* and *Ariel* would be found guilty of incompetence at a court-martial. By this point, John may have wished he had stayed on the *William Black*.

While John busied himself with the merchant service and his social life, the Royal Navy had not completely escaped his attention, although there was a growing edge of resentment, as his letters show. John was proud of his naval exploits, but he had not received the promotion or recognition that he and those around him felt he deserved. He had given many years of service to the Navy, during a time when Britain was constantly at war, with all the brutal encounters, sacrifice, injury, and hardship that involved. He continued to wear his full dress uniform to formal social events and enjoyed the respect he commanded locally around Neston and Parkgate, where he was supposedly known locally as 'Nelson', due to his naval background, one good eye and damaged arm.[11]

Through the years that followed Algiers, he had made several attempts to put his case to the Admiralty, often with the support of influential friends. In 1820, after John and his brother Charles had rescued General Grosvenor from his carriage on the Old Dee Bridge, John received an offer of help from the Grosvenor family at a Chester election meeting. Seizing the opportunity, John wrote to Richard Grosvenor and described his naval service, giving particular attention to the attack on Algiers. He was unusually poetic in his description of events:

It's no use taking up your time presenting the particulars of that dreadful battle. All I can boast is that I belonged to the ship that had the Post of Honour, and dreadful was the havoc made on board and I was wounded in three places in that glorious affair which released so many unfortunate wretches to their last farewell.

He went on to explain what he saw as the injustice he had been done by the Admiralty in overlooking him for promotion to commander:

It is well known that the Admiralty did not behave well in only appointing one Lieutenant for promotion (which was the First) at the same time even the small brigs had one appointed. Lord Melville's view was that the proper number of officers was already appointed by the Admiralty and was sorry he could not comply with their wishes... Only for the great encouragement I receive from my old commanders I certainly would have entered into another service.[12]

John added that he hoped to get his name onto the list of promotions at George IV's coronation and ended forlornly with 'I have served my country above 14 years'.

The 'First' to whom John refers was James Boyle Babbington, the first lieutenant on the *Impregnable*, who had been promoted to commander immediately on his return from Algiers in September 1816. In the years since, John had watched as other peers had also been promoted. Roger Hall, a lieutenant who had served alongside him on both the *Berwick* and *Impregnable*, had made commander in 1819, and Francis Brace had been promoted first to commander in 1818 and then to captain in 1827. The world was moving on while John languished as a lieutenant.

The well-intentioned encouragement from his family may have made it harder to put the matter behind him. In 1827, his brother-in-law Edward Acton Gibbon encouraged John to press his case again with the Admiralty. 'Don't let it lie!'[13] he said, before adding that he was out of cigars and would be grateful for a new straw hat. Buoyed by this support, John tried again. He wrote to his old captain, Edward Brace, at the United Services Club, to request a letter of commendation. Having heard nothing back, John asked for help from John Lloyd, Parkgate regular and regatta organiser, but more importantly, also a Chester solicitor who had worked on the Luddite trials with the former Home Secretary, Lord Sidmouth. Lloyd chased around London on John's behalf and called at Brace's club, where he learned that John's letter lay waiting among other unopened post. When finally contacted, Brace provided the letter of commendation for which John had hoped, praising his 'zeal and gallantry'. This was passed to Richard Grosvenor, who duly forwarded the commendation to the Duke of Clarence, the future King William IV, and Lord High Admiral at this time.[14]

The papers which John left behind present an extraordinary catalogue of schemes and stratagems to approach the great and the good of British society. John's situation was common, however, and each person he approached was likely receiving a steady stream of similar requests.

Lloyd and John also proposed to have his petition or 'memorial' certified by Lord Exmouth. Lloyd spoke to Lord Sidmouth, who tried to approach Exmouth on the matter, but found that he was out of town. John's memorial appeared to have been presented to the Lord High Admiral already by this point, but Sidmouth recommended that John write directly to Exmouth with his request, or that Grosvenor write on his behalf so if John had already sailed. Whichever approach was ultimately settled upon, the result was similarly unsuccessful.

At about the same time, in a separate action, the Mayor of Chester and the city corporation also petitioned the Lords of the Admiralty for John's promotion. Algiers had been a source of national pride and, like every city, Chester was proud of its local participants. Elsewhere, letters indicate that John's supporters also took his claim to other influential politicians at this time, among them George Canning and William Huskisson.[15]

With the weight of all these prominent figures on his side, John must have felt heartened that his claim for promotion would be successful, but he seems to have met with nothing but delays and vague assurances. These were good connections to have made but, again, they somehow failed to bear fruit.

A return to sea

Alongside the social engagements of 1829 and his pursuit of promotion, John Monk also spent the year planning his return to sea. He had built a network of business relationships in Liverpool, Dublin and Leghorn throughout the 1820s, and with the support of his agent, George Yates, John intended to return to the southern trading routes he knew so well.

In need of a new command, he headed 120 miles north, to Maryport and the yard of Kelsick Wood. Kelsick was a ship-builder who ran his yard with his sons on the Solway Firth, Cumbria, from where they launched between two and three merchant vessels a year, mainly brigs and sloops. The family business had been active in Maryport since 1765, the first to arrive in the town, and worked in all aspects of shipbuilding and ship rigging.

At the time of John's approach in 1829, Kelsick's yard in North Harbour had a brig on the blocks called the *General Gascoyne*, named after one of Liverpool's two sitting MPs. She had not yet been registered, and when John came forward to purchase her, he renamed her to the *Monk*.[16]

John's new brig first hit the water on February 10th, 1830. Once launched, it took another three months before she was fully rigged and fitted out, and John finally received his certif-icate of registry in Liverpool on May 12th.

The *Monk* was seventy-seven feet long, with a beam width of twenty-two feet and a hold fourteen feet deep, giving her a burthen weight of 170 tons. She had one deck and two masts, with a copper-sheathed hull, to give greater speed by protecting it from shipworm and weed growth. She had been brig-rigged, with a standing bowsprit and square stern. Building ships was a hugely timber-intensive business, and Kelsick's supply chain was diverse and international. The *Monk* was built from native British oak, African teak imported from Millicourie on the Guinea coast, as well as beech and birch from Scotland, elm from the Crimea, and red, yellow and pitch pine from Quebec.[17]

Ahead of her first voyage in 1830, she was advertised as having 'superior accommodation for passengers, and as being expected to sail remarkably fast',[18] although similar boasts appear on most listings from this era. Being considerably larger than the *William Black*, it took a larger crew to sail her. The mate and crew of ten were entirely different from those John had employed previously. Michael Kearney and William Dalgleish were mate on voyages between 1830 and 1832, before David Hillier took over in 1833. Hillier would remain with the ship until her rocky demise.

Records show that John took the *Monk* to the Mediterranean nine times over the next six years. On most voyages he made Leghorn his first port of call, returning to Liverpool via Dublin. Not everything in the official record is as it seems at first glance, though, and dates don't always align. In April 1831, John requested six months' leave from the Admiralty to visit the Gulf of St Lawrence, Quebec and Montreal, and the following October, he wrote to inform them that he had returned from Canada. Peculiarly, shipping records show that during those same summer months, the *Monk,* with John Monk named as master, made a fairly uneventful visit to Gibraltar and Cadiz, all carefully and consistently recorded in *Lloyd's List* and *Gore's Liverpool Advertiser.* It may be that circumstances had forced him to cancel his trip to Canada at short notice, but, if that is the case, it suggests a growing disdain for the Admiralty, in that he concluded that it was easier to complete the original story than to explain to them that his plans had changed.

In January 1836, John sent the *Monk* to sea with a different master, while he remained at home. It was a step into the unknown and would likely have caused him some initial anxiety. John put his trust in Thomas Herbert, formerly of the *Hope*, to take charge in his absence. Herbert and the *Monk* left Liverpool on January 1st for Leghorn and were back in Dublin by the end of June, the trip having been uneventful. John was seemingly acquiring a liking for life on land, and when the *Monk* was made ready for her next voyage, he appointed his mate Hillier as master.

Many years later, when his nephew William Brown delivered the speech in Peel town hall about his Uncle John's life, William referred to this voyage, although he mistakenly placed it in 1844.[19] His uncle had told William that he had given Hillier the command through necessity. The brig was supposedly already loaded with cargo, but John himself had not received the necessary papers to leave the United Kingdom, due to an unspecified foreign complication. Another account suggests that John did not have a master's licence or 'ticket', which the government was introducing as it sought to regulate the industry. This seems mistaken, though, as the master's licence was not compulsory until 1850, and, as an experienced master mariner, John would have been eligible to apply for a certificate of service and not have had to sit an examination. Whatever the truth behind this, John seems to have shown very little interest in getting back out to sea after 1836.

By July the following year, Hillier and the crew were beginning their journey home. They had departed from Liverpool in September 1836 and sailed first to Leghorn. From there they had left the Mediterranean, crossed the Atlantic and arrived in the Caribbean in late February, where they delivered their cargo at St Domingo. They had then headed back across the Atlantic, returning to Leghorn in June 1837. Hillier and his crew had travelled further and been away for longer than John had chosen to do during his own merchant career. They had spent a month or more at each port, waiting while their cargo was unloaded and new freight was brought on board. Most recently, the *Monk* had left Leghorn for the second and final time on July 15th and was heading back to Liverpool via Cork, a round trip of almost a year, when it all went wrong.

It was a bright, sunny morning on Monday, July 31st and HMS *Dido* was at anchor in Malaga Roads. The ship's company were scrubbing hammocks and washing clothes when the captain got a report that an English merchant brig was in trouble nearby. The captain and crew prepared for sea, and by the afternoon they reached the stranded vessel, the *Monk*, which had run aground on a rocky beach.[20]

The *Dido*'s captain sent one of the ship's boats to see what assistance they could offer and, the next day, he ordered an officer and a party of seamen to assist the crew in moving anything salvageable onto shore. By the end of the day, the *Dido* had received anchors, cables, and 148 boxes of oil from the wreck. A sergeant and six marines were posted on the beach to guard the remaining cargo. On Wednesday morning, with salvageable items safely stowed, Hillier and his crew of ten also came on board. The *Dido* then weighed anchor and set sail for Malaga.

On arrival at Malaga, the crew of HMS *Dido* spent Thursday and Friday unloading the brig's stores and cargo. Hillier and the crew disembarked and made their way to Gibraltar, where they were stuck for two weeks until a furious John Monk, as the ship's owner, arranged their return to Liverpool.

The crew returned home to find John an angry man, in no mood to pay the wages they were owed. John would have blamed a basic lack of judgment by Hillier for the loss of his vessel. It had been a dark night, with a cloudy sky and no moon, but in the middle of summer, when sailing conditions were good. The weather was fine, the winds were gentle, and the sea was calm.

To darken John's mood further, part of the owners' insurance claim appears to have been challenged by the underwriters. In an undated letter, Emma de Blois Russell, sister of John's former sweetheart Sally, offered him some encouragement:

I am very happy to hear that you are likely to recover each a part of your insurance & I have a message for you on that subject. Mr. Clarke begs me to say that he has thought much on the subject of your loss and he is satisfied that, if you would try, you would gain all the insurance. He consulted Mr Whateley the other night who perfectly agreed with him. And they are both sensible and thinking men. I should place much dependence on their opinions.[21]

With the crew's wages still unpaid, John received a summons from Andrew Hutton, the ship's former chief mate. The case was heard at Liverpool Police Court on Wednesday, September 20th, with Mr Hall presiding. Reports in Liverpool newspapers are contradictory on some points, but the longer, more detailed account appeared in *Gore's Liverpool General Advertiser*.

Hutton said that he had shipped on board John's brig in Liverpool as chief mate and signed articles for wages of £4 4s per month. He claimed that the ship's company were entitled to wages up to the moment when the vessel was lost on July 30th, and that John, therefore, owed him £16 in unpaid wages. The men also claimed salvage, as part of the cargo had been saved, and they were upset that, after their rescue by HMS *Dido*, they had been left waiting for fifteen days in Gibraltar before John found a ship to bring them home.

When invited to respond, John grumbled that his ship 'was a total wreck, and the articles had been lost with her'. For his part, he said, he had 'no hesitation to pay such proportion of the wages as are actually due, but the crew object to every proposal and will not be satisfied.' The two weeks' wait in Gibraltar, John said, was because he could not get a vessel to convey the crew away any sooner. In answer to their claim for salvage, John stated that 'There had not been ten-penceworth of goods saved out the vessel'.

This last statement may show why this dispute had ended up in court and hints that John's treatment of his former crew was not quite as fair as he sought to portray. To claim that no goods of value had been saved was, at best, an exaggeration, given that the log of HMS *Dido* records that her crew had spent two days recovering cargo from the *Monk* and then unloading it at Malaga.

In his judgement, Hall seems generally to have sided with John. The seamen were told to calculate their wages up to the date of discharge of cargo at Leghorn in June, minus any advances received. They were not entitled to salary after that date, as the brig had been lost on her homeward voyage to Cork and had not 'earned a freight' or completed her delivery. Hall also denied their salvage claim and said he had seen no proof of unnecessary detentions in Gibraltar. Hutton said he considered this judgement very hard.

The balance of Hall's judgements had been in John's favour, but any celebrations would likely have been bitter sweet. The verdict did not change the fact that he had lost his ship and his main source of income.[22]

The wrecking of the *Monk* in 1837 seems to have marked the end of John Monk's career as an active mariner. He was 46 at this time and found himself at an unexpected crossroads. If he were to return to sea, John would need to start over again, and either agree to command a vessel of which he was not owner, or invest in a new merchant brig, with the financial commitment that would entail. The purchase of the *William Black* and the *Monk* had been expensive and to maintain them in a seaworthy state would have involved a continual outflow of funds.

The seeds of change may already have been there, though. Over the last couple of years, John had shown a willingness to send his vessel out under the command of a different master, first with Thomas Herbert and then, to his eternal regret, with David Hillier. Aside from the dangers of storm and ship-wreck, thirty years at sea will take its toll on any man. Years before, John had seen how his captain, James Macnamara, had suffered from fevers and rheumatism, exacerbated by the wind, the cold and the near-constant dampness that accompanied life on a Georgian sailing vessel. The later years of

John's life would show an increasing contentment at home in his garden, and it may be that his desire to return to sea had simply left him.

John's decision may also have been influenced by the technological changes he saw in the world around him. It was now fifty years since the first steam vessels had been trialled, and John had borne witness to the slow but steady shift from sail to steam that had begun to take place. Sail did not lose its appeal overnight but, in the decades that followed John's withdrawal from the merchant service, a string of inventions and improvements made steam power increasingly attractive, and by the 1850s, steamers dominated routes between Liverpool and the Mediterranean.

Politicians and other dignitaries were often keen to get a closer view of the Liverpool docks, so central to Britain's prosperity, and steam ships were clearly part of the attraction. On occasion, John offered his services as tour guide. Writing from his home in Warrington, John Wilson Patten, the Conservative MP, thanked John for his offer to tour the steamships at Liverpool but said he had recently visited and been out on the *Liverpool* steamer.[23] On a separate occasion, one Saturday in October 1838, a year after the wrecking of the *Monk*, John returned to Liverpool with his former agent George Yates, where they gave a tour of the docks and town to the visiting Turkish ambassador, 'with which his excellency expressed himself much delighted'. The ambassador was then taken on a tour in the steamer HMS *Redwing*, with the Turkish flag flying at the main. They left the Prince's Pier, sailed close to the *Liverpool* steamer, round the lazarettos and continued a few miles beyond the Rock lighthouse, by which time the ambassador was 'exceedingly delighted'.[24]

Although he would never again take personal charge of a ship at sea, John continued to deal with shipping agents to place cargo on vessels that passed through Liverpool.

One of the first merchant vessels on which John sent goods after the sinking of the *Monk* was the schooner *Wild Irish Girl*, through agents McNair and Dutton. She had a frustrating and expensive start to her maiden voyage in October 1837, which brought John back to court for the second time in two months. The *Wexford Independent* described in detail the events that unfolded, and the legal dispute which inevitably followed.[25]

Wild Irish Girl left Liverpool on October 7th under the command of William Tooker, bound for Trieste carrying what was termed 'general cargo', mainly baled goods such as cotton and linen, with John Monk's shipments among them. Four days into her journey, as she passed the south-eastern coast of Ireland, she ran aground on Blackwater Bank off the County Wexford coast. The bank was a notorious spot for shipwrecks. Over the years, there had been regular calls for a lighthouse but as of 1837 nothing had been done. *Wild Irish Girl's* hull scraped her way across the sand bank and refloated but, with damage to her rudder and keel, she was trapped in an area of shallow water. The captain later claimed that he had not been unduly concerned, as the hull was not leaking, the weather was reasonable, and the sea was not particularly rough. His problem was a practical one only, as the ship was too heavily laden to pass back over the bank.

Tooker sent the ship's boats ashore that night to ask for help.

There was no shortage of volunteers, but how much help any of them provided would later be decided in court. The first to arrive the following morning were the coastguards, who said their role was to remain on board until the situation had been resolved. They settled into the master's cabin, smoked, and found a bottle of rum. Rather more helpfully, they alerted William Powell, a local man who operated as an unofficial agent of the shipping underwriters, with instructions to aid any vessel in distress. Powell knew the coast well, and when he was made aware of the situation, he sent for the local steamer, *Town of Wexford*, which spent the day taking on board part of the schooner's cargo. Powell then inspected the damaged rudder and hired a passing schooner, the *Sarah Jane*, to tow the lightened vessel off the bank and to safety in South Bay where repairs could be undertaken.

In the days that followed, salvage claims appeared from all those who had attended the scene, regardless of the role they had played, even the coastguard boatmen who had spent the day getting drunk in the master's cabin. A successful salvor was legally entitled to a reward, and everyone wanted to be part of it. A lengthy five-day inquiry began on Tuesday, October 31st in a crowded room at the custom house in Cork. John Monk arrived to represent the Liverpool merchants, along with the agent, Samuel Dutton, who appears to have done most of the talking. The largest claims came from the owner and agent of the Wexford steamer and from Mr Powell, who had guided the ship over the bank to safety.

Speaking for the Liverpool agent and merchants, Mr Dutton was in no mood to be generous. He began his argument by stating that he and Monk 'wanted nothing but justice', but then went on to dismantle each claim, one by one. Firstly, he said, this was not a salvage case at all. *Wild Irish Girl* had not been in real danger and Tooker had the time and inclination simply to hire the services he needed. Dutton dismissed smaller claimants as no more than 'scene shifters and candle snuffers'. He was still more damning of Mr Powell: 'In short, gentlemen, it does appear to me that he was not wanted and that he rendered no assistance for which he should be remunerated.' He accepted that the steamer had assisted them but said it was not salvage work, just shifting cargo. Master of the steamer, Jemmy Howlin, who was loud and badly behaved throughout the hearing, muttered, 'Thank God we have the goods', suggesting John's cargo might not be returned unless salvage claims were settled to his satisfaction.

In defence of Powell's claim, Counsellor Alcock spoke generally about the benefits of the salvage system. Traditionally, poor coastal communities like those around Wexford had considered anything lost from a ship to be fair game and had seen nothing morally wrong with plundering shipwrecks. It was only in more recent years that the rule of salvage law had been strictly enforced. Rewarding salvage efforts was important, otherwise 'you will revive that barbarous system of plunder which formerly prevailed on this coast.'[26]

The magistrates gave their verdict on Saturday afternoon. Substantial awards were made to the *Town of Wexford* steamer and Mr Powell, although each was smaller than the amount claimed. The drunken coastguards left with their heads hung in shame – they had claimed £300 and were awarded just £20.

The picture of John Monk's merchant business after 1838 becomes fragmented and harder to follow. Surviving records of Liverpool merchants and shipping agents are not as complete or as accessible as those recording the movement of naval or merchant ships and their crew. There are indications, though, of how long this merchant career lasted. When William O'Byrne was preparing his monumental biography of every living British naval officer, he requested information directly from the officers in question either by interview or by letter. The entry for John, to which we can assume he contributed, says that he finally retired as a merchant in 1844, aged 53.

8. The comforts of home

The Georgian era was drawing to a close just as John Monk retired as a mariner. William IV, the Sailor King, had died in June 1837 and, in June 1838, Neston and Parkgate joined the rest of the country in celebrating the coronation of Queen Victoria. The townsfolk gathered to watch as fireworks were launched from the top of the church tower, before John, now 47, and brother Charles, 57, fired a cannon in the meadow to announce the coronation of 'Victoria the Good'.[1]

John and Charles seem to have rubbed along with each other well enough through the years, but there are few indications that they were particularly close, not in the way John was to his sisters Elizabeth and Nessie. His brother was a different kind of man. Letters and other reports show Charles to be eloquent and civil, and someone who placed great store in his reputation as a pillar of the local community. John's life had taken him on a different path. Decades at sea had imbued him with a tough and independent temperament. He could hold his own in the company of Cheshire's gentry, but there are occasional indications that he had retained a certain roughness in his manner. His matter-of-fact advice to a friend with dental pain suggests he may also have been influenced by his encounters with Royal Navy surgeons:

I hope this will find your tooth better. If not, do as I do, discharge it.[2]

Such problems while at sea on the *William Black* or the

Monk would have left John with little choice, but it is hard to picture his brother Charles or friend Richard Grosvenor recommending the same quite so bluntly!

Parkgate's lustre was fading as Victoria ascended to the throne. Leisure activities like sea bathing had previously been a pastime for wealthy Georgians but now became something open to the whole of society, due in part to the improving road network and the rise of the railway. Doctors increasingly recommended trips to seaside resorts to all of their patients, not just the wealthy, where fresh sea air could provide an escape from the choking pollution of industrialised cities. The seaside became a destination for the masses, and larger, more commercialised resorts like New Brighton and Llandudno grew up to cater for their needs. Parkgate began to seem rather quaint and increasingly neglected in comparison.

Without the formal structure of shipping reports and captain's logs, the record of John Monk's life on land becomes a composite of abstracted moments frozen in newspaper articles, personal letters and other records, much of which seems to involve his garden. Having spent many of the previous thirty summers in foreign ports or at sea as a busy mariner, John seems to have enjoyed the peaceful times at home, sitting shaded from the summer sun, admiring the greenery in the garden around him. He had friends nearby and enjoyed their company, among them George Louthean, a Liverpool ship-owner and former colleague of his agent, the late George Yates. The casual and relaxed tone is apparent in John's letters:

Nice piece of roast beef for dinner on Sunday if you and Mr Cross feel inclined for a walk, glad of your company. Sorry to hear about poor Mr W Shand. No news here of him yet being found.[3]

In July 1843, the *Liverpool Mail* and several other newspapers reported that Captain Monk, R.N., 'has in his garden at Neston a rose tree of a peculiar species, which at this time bears 3,700 flowers, besides innumerable buds to come in succession'.[4] It is a trivial but restful glimpse of domestic life in Parkgate Road, with John taking the time to count or calculate the number of flowers in front of him.

Old habits die hard. John retained the naval officer's routine of keeping detailed logs of the world around him, although that world was now as viewed from his garden. He kept a careful meteorological log, checked his barometer regularly, and made notes on air temperature, general conditions and, of course, wind speed.

The night sky was at least partially clear for the lunar eclipse on Sunday, November 24th, 1844. John stood in his garden, with the chill quiet of the November night around him as he peered at the stars through his spyglass. With a mariner's knowledge of the night sky, John would have been in his element. He wrote to the *Chester Chronicle* with a careful account of what he saw:

I observed this eclipse at Neston, Sunday 24th November, with a common spyglass. The day had been very fine, and the moon rose clear and bright at six: the firmament was extensively obscured with cumulus which continued for some time, but still, I was able to observe the beginning and end of the eclipse... At the middle of the eclipse, the moon's appearance was of a dark copper colour or more like old mahogany, and the beautiful ring near the verge of the shadow, had a still lighter or orangy colour appearance. The whole sky was very clear, and the stars extremely bright. The night was calm and frosty, the thermometer in the garden at midnight 31½. The moon was N. of the eclipse between Taurus and the Pleiades. John Monk, Lt R.N., Neston 26th 1844.[5]

Despite these scenes of domestic tranquillity, there are signs elsewhere that John's lack of progression within the Royal Navy remained an irritation to him. Arguably, it should no longer have mattered. In the decades since he had last seen active service, he had been a successful ship-owner, a master mariner and a merchant, although it may be that retirement now gave him time to dwell on these things. Despite his best and repeated efforts, he remained a lieutenant on half-pay, and he was sensitive about what he saw as his limited circumstances.

Throughout the 1820s and 1830s, John had nurtured his friendship with Richard Grosvenor. The two men were of a similar age, and since 1818 they had met regularly at social events around Cheshire. John had routinely returned with gifts from his Mediterranean travels, ranging from liqueurs for Grosvenor to exotic seeds for his wife, Elizabeth.[6]

Richard Grosvenor was a valuable ally, and one who repeatedly represented his friend's interests to the Lords of the Admiralty, as John continued to press for the promotion to captain that he believed he deserved. The friendship endured despite social differences. Grosvenor was a hereditary lord and a hugely wealthy and influential landowner, whereas John was a naval lieutenant on half-pay. John was no aristocrat, but he was a charismatic, well-travelled man who had faced death and survived dangers of which Grosvenor had no experience.

Being friends with the richest man in England undoubtedly had its benefits, but became problematic when that friendship strayed into discussion of business and employment. A well-intentioned, if clumsy, invitation from Grosvenor to John, not long after the sinking of the *Monk*, seems to have triggered a rather petulant and emotional response.

In 1840, Grosvenor was excited about the arrival of his new yacht, the *Dolphin*, a large, 217-ton schooner. She was a sleek, elegant vessel and had already won the Queen's Plate at Cowes in 1838. Needing a skipper, he invited John to command her for him and offered a salary that he believed to be appropriate. The move backfired badly. John felt insulted by Grosvenor's offer, perhaps upset that Grosvenor appeared to have assigned a monetary value to their friendship, and a rather low one at that. He wrote to Grosvenor that he felt the salary offered was 'considerably under' what he would expect, 'being not much above half what is paid at Liverpool'. Grosvenor was a wealthy but prudent man and made enquiries with other members at the Royal Yacht Squadron. He replied to John by letter that his offer was broadly in line with what others were paying and signed off by pointedly, wishing him 'the enjoyment of your comfortable cottage'.[7]

John responded gruffly that he was prepared to overlook the inadequacy of the salary and accept the role of master, out of regard and kindness for Grosvenor, but in a tone that put them both into a still more uncomfortable position. The whole discussion had become an awkward embarrassment for both men, and Grosvenor retracted his offer. He told John he had received a recommendation for a different skipper, a Mr Leese, and his irritation at his friend was clear:

I sincerely hope that you have not put yourself to any inconvenience during the short time our negociation had been pending and

I also most sincerely regret that out of regard for one, you should for an instant have been tempted to think of leaving the comforts of home.[8]

Two months later, in August, the *Dolphin* was being painted in Southampton. Tempers had cooled and each man made efforts to calm the waters. John offered to lend Grosvenor his chronometer, and Grosvenor visited the Admiralty again to press John's case for promotion, but the awkwardness between them seems to have remained.[9]

Grosvenor would have been too busy to dwell on the argument for long. He and his wife Elizabeth left Plymouth on the *Dolphin* in October 1840 and did not return to England until November 1841. They toured the Mediterranean extensively, made lengthy excursions into Portugal, Spain, Morocco, and Italy and sailed east to Turkey and Greece, both countries to which John's travels had never taken him.

It may be that John later regretted letting his pride and insecurities get the better of him, but there was probably some truth in Grosvenor's digs. John does indeed seem to have been quite content in his 'comfortable cottage' on Parkgate Road and perhaps had no real desire to go back to sea. Be that as it may, Elizabeth Grosvenor later published her travel journals in two volumes in 1842, and it is hard to read them without feeling frustration that John's stubborn pride meant he had not been on board.[10]

Despite the gestures both men made to mend their disagreement, no further personal notes survive, and their friendship appears to have cooled. Gifts of game continued to be presented to John each Christmas by the Grosvenors, but the notes were sent by servants, in the third person only:

Lord Westminster sends a line to Capt Monk to appraise him that he hopes to have the pleasure of sending to his address, on Saturday next, with all the good wishes of the season, a haunch of Doe Venison, killed on the 17th of December and a brace of pheasants, which will be left for the Carrier.[11]

There were other aspects of his new life at home that may have hastened the end of John's days at sea, and which meant he had not embraced Grosvenor's offer more eagerly. Without the long absences, John was able to spend more time with his siblings and their often sprawling families. Among the Monk brothers, only Whitehouse had had children, while his sisters had produced twenty sons and daughters between them.

Earlier in life, each time John had returned home from his naval ship or from his latest voyage on the *William Black*, his parents are likely to have greeted him with an excited rush of family news, with talk of marriages, grandchildren and future plans. Now, however, as John adjusted to a life on land at the beginning of the Victorian age, he was to be present for much of the sadness that followed. Every family will experience grief over the years, but his sisters Arabella and Elizabeth suffered more than most mothers must bear.

Arabella had stayed in the Parkgate area and married a local surgeon, John Wharton Bankes, in 1825. They made their home on Neston High Street, opposite the church and just a short walk from her brothers, John, Charles and Joseph, when they were not at sea. Her husband was well regarded in the community, and Arabella was the proud mother of three young children, Nessie, James Roger and Arabella Ann, born between 1827 and 1831. Elizabeth visited Arabella after her first daughter Nessie's birth in 1827, and wrote to John,

I am sure you were delighted to see Bell's little girl. Don't think I ever saw a nicer child.[12]

The young couple's joy was to be short lived, however, as death came repeatedly to Arabella's family in the 1840s. Two of her three children died between 1844 and 1845, and her husband was also taken from her not long after, with her third child following them in 1854. Death certificates show that all were victims of tuberculosis, or consumption as it was known. The disease was the single largest killer of the nineteenth century. It accounted for more than twenty percent of all deaths in the first half of the century and claimed a disproportionately high number of younger victims. It was typically a disease of the lungs. Initial flu-like symptoms would give way to a severe cough, the spitting up of blood as the inflamed lungs began to lesion, anaemia, weight loss and muscle wastage. The decline could take years, with periods of remission and relapse, and sufferers were left thin, pale, and weak. The disease gained the name the White Death and was a major influence on Romantic artists and writers like Byron and Shelley, who romanticized sufferers' ghostly pallor and listlessness as tragic and melancholic.

Seventy-five miles to the east of Neston, at their home at Haworth Parsonage, the Brontë family was facing a similar trauma. Two of the five Brontë sisters, Maria and Elizabeth, had died from tuberculosis while at school in 1825. The year after Arabella Bankes had buried her husband John in Neston in 1847, across the Pennines, Charlotte Brontë lost her sister Emily and brother Branwell to the same disease, before Anne succumbed the following year. The disease was bacterial, spread by airborne particles in a cough or a sneeze, which accounts for the way it would often take several members of a family, as it had with Arabella's. None of this was understood in 1847, although there was a growing recognition that nutrition and fresh air were beneficial. The bacillus that caused the disease would finally be identified in 1882, but an effective treatment remained out of reach until the discovery of penicillin in 1928.

Life in the merchant service had taken John regularly to Dublin. Over the years, much of his time on land between voyages had been spent in the district of Sandymount with his sister Elizabeth, her husband Edward and their children. After 1820, each of these visits would have been something of a family reunion, as his youngest sister, Nessie, was also nearby. Nessie had married a friend of her brother-in-law and a fellow Irishman from Sandymount, Mervyn Matthews, who ran his family's timber business.

Having no children of his own, John appears to have been a particularly attentive uncle. When Elizabeth's daughter, Nessie Gibbon, died in 1837 aged 23, John was distraught. He broke the news by letter to his nephew, William Brown in Chester, and for a hardened Navy veteran, who had repeatedly seen death at close quarters, it is touching to see the depth of John's emotion:

My hand and heart still flutter so much that the task of writing is almost impossible for last night I got a letter from Mr G saying how much better she was. It's like a dream. I can hardly believe it.[13]

John helped to return Nessie's body to Dublin, where, honouring her final wish, she was buried at St Mark's Church, next to her sister Maryann, who had been laid to rest just the previous year. The girls' deaths were just two of many faced by Elizabeth and Edward at this time, with tuberculosis once more likely to have been responsible. By 1842, Elizabeth herself and eight of her nine children had died, none of the children seeing their fortieth birthday. From this large Irish family, only her husband Edward and son William Monk Gibbon remained.

The last Monk sister was Ann, who, viewed through Georgian eyes, had married well. Her husband, John Brown, was a successful auctioneer in Chester, from a family that already had wealth and influence, and whose fortunes would increase greatly through the Regency and Victorian years.[14] The Brown family's drapery and haberdashery business had grown fast, moved to larger premises on Eastgate Street and would in time evolve into the Browns of Chester department store, heralded in the Victorian years as the 'Harrods of the North'.[15]

Ann, her husband, and their children lived in Flookersbrook, an attractive hamlet on the approach to the city, with large, elegant houses and spacious gardens. Willow trees leant over a pond by the road, near to a 'good looking tavern called the Ermine',[16] of which her brother Whitehouse would be the ill-fated proprietor for a short time.

John Brown's auction business thrived. Each sale was advertised in the *Chester Chronicle*, which gives a good insight into how busy he was. On November 20th, 1845, he was at the Albion Hotel, auctioning horses and carriages. The following evening, he was at the Hop-Pole Inn, selling the Golden Lion Inn on Foregate Street and other plots of land. A week later, on December 2nd, he was at the Exchange in Chester, auctioning the right to collect rent on all the city's market stalls.[17]

In contrast to her sisters, Arabella and Elizabeth, who could only watch as their families withered and died, Ann's children flourished, untouched by nineteenth-century diseases like tuberculosis or smallpox. Two of the boys, William (1816-1900) and Charles (1818-1900), would serve as mayor of Chester, as two of their uncles had done earlier in the century. Among John Monk's many nephews and nieces, it is William who appears to have been especially fond of him. It was William who arranged John's care in his later years as his health failed, William who gave the eulogies after his death and William who gathered together John's personal papers, on which much of this account is based.

Ann's eldest child, Nessie Brown (1814-1905), was John's goddaughter and would be one of the founders of The Queen's School, Chester. A surviving letter from Nessie also provides a degree of closure to the story of her uncle's friendship with the Massone family in Genoa.

In 1869, fifty-five years after a young Lieutenant Monk had rescued an even younger Teresa Massone from the band of ruffians, Nessie Brown found herself in Genoa on business. She decided to look up the Massone family she knew from the colourful tales told by her uncle, who at this time was at home in Parkgate Road, approaching his eightieth year. It took some effort for Nessie to locate the family and, when she called at the address she had been given, she was disappointed to find no one home.

A few days later, though, on the evening of Tuesday, March 16th, she was visited by Marietta Massone, the widow of Teresa's brother Carlo, together with her two sons, Francesco and

Tommaso, and her nephew Amiti, the eldest son of Norina. The meeting seems to have been enjoyable and Marietta did her best to fill in events in the intervening half-century. Nessie learned that Teresa had died by this time, but that the letters she had received as a young girl from the smart young naval officer were still carefully preserved by the family in the box he had given her.[18] Whether that little box and its letters have also survived the next 150 years is a mystery yet to be solved.

In January 1848, John was visited at home by old friends, Wilson-Patten, Sir John Yarde Buller and Lady Buller, who was also Wilson-Patten's sister. As John later recounted in an unhappy letter to George Louthean, in which he glumly refers to his provincial home as 'Dusty Corner', comments made by Lady Buller had left him feeling humiliated at his lowly position:

One miserable cold wet day, the later end of January, I was taken all aback with a visit from Sir John Yarde Buller, Lady Buller, and Sir John, Wilson Patten M.P. also came from Bank Hall Warrington to see me in Dusty Corner. I had not seen them for 20 years and they were much surprised to find me a poor half-pay Lieut. Lady B said in a laughing way, she expected to find me an admiral.[19]

John explained his thwarted attempts at promotion to them and lamented that he would settle for being made a commander on the retirement list. Wilson-Patten told him that he should present his case to the sitting MP, Edward Mostyn, who was to visit Parkgate on March 1st and who, he assured John, was close to the Lords of the Admiralty.

That evening, John's guests had left but the impact of Lady

B's words had clearly remained. After all his entreaties to the Admiralty, John was clearly pained by his lack of promotion, and, whether they had been unthinking or unkind, Lady Buller's comments spurred John, now 56, to have another try.

John knew that time was not on his side, and that this might be his final opportunity. He asked Charles to assist, but his brother was unsympathetic:

Having no friend in this neighbourhood to assist me, I asked Mr Monk. He said his eyes was bad and it was all nonsense and refused.

Undeterred, though increasingly unwell with the flu, John stayed up all night, in a state of some agitation, and drafted yet another service history. Needing assistance and suitable stationery, John turned to Louthean to ask for help and a large sheet of paper, as there was apparently none to be had in Neston:

So I now take the liberty if you will correct it, prune it and make it as best you can, and to ask Mr Scott if he will please to copy it out for me on a long sheet of paper, and to let me have back on or before Thursday morning, for it is sure to go before the Lords of the Admiralty… Please excuse all the mistakes and the trouble I am giving you, for I feel so bothered, & my eyes so bad I don't know what I am doing. I'm not fit for any business.[20]

Louthean seems to have been a useful source for all manner of things: a few months later, John asked him for a sack of Lancashire pink-eye seed potatoes as he and Joseph had taken a plot of land.

Together the two men prepared a summary of John's career for him to present to Mostyn on his visit, although, with increasing recognition of the hopelessness of his cause, John acknowledged to Louthean that he felt that he had exhausted possible avenues:

All my old commanders are dead, I have not a friend left in the Navy that I can apply for advice.

When the appointed day in March came, however, Mostyn visited as planned but the two men did not get to speak. The only option now was to send it by post. Mostyn responded that he would happily present John's application to the Admiralty, but after thirty years of setbacks and disappointment, John's expectations were understandably low, and he seemed to share his brother Charles' grumpy pessimism:

I am sorry to say the Hon. Mr Mostyn never came near us. I sent the memorial upon the 3rd inst. and he kindly wrote to say he would have great pleasure in submitting it to the Lords of the Admiralty. I shall not be disappointed for I don't expect their Lordships will pay any attention to it... It will be the last trial I shall ever make but having been so long out of the service I am afraid it will be a hopeless cause.

As the surviving Monk siblings grew older, their worlds grew steadily smaller. Except for Ann, who had remained in the house in Flookersbrook after her husband's sudden death in 1846, the five remaining Monks were childless and turned increasingly back towards each other for practical and emotional support. As the sole beneficiary of their father William's estate, and with his sizeable portfolio of local properties, it may have been understood within the family that Charles had a duty to provide financial assistance or accommodation for his siblings where needed.

After his retirement from the customs service, Charles decided it was time to build himself a new house, once again on Parkgate Road, Neston. The Cottage, since renamed to Beech House, is an attractive, well-proportioned, two-storey structure, set back from the road. Not content just to scratch his name on a window as he had done at The Hermitage, Charles positioned a small tablet over the porch, inscribed and dated 'C.M. 1847'. He was joined in his new house by his sister Arabella, now widowed and childless.

John and Nessie were their close neighbours. Nessie had returned from Dublin, also a widow, and by 1851 she was living with her brother, most probably in one of the many houses Charles owned. John and Nessie shared their home for the next twenty-five years, employing a succession of young local women, Sarah, Hannah and Jane, as resident domestic servants, to ease the burden of managing the household.

Their brother Joseph was also close by, in Back Lane, where he lived alone with his house servant, Maria. Joseph had never married and had joked in an 1826 letter that he had seen enough of his brother's marriage not to be tempted. After Joseph's death from heart disease in 1857, his four ageing siblings remained as they were for the last twenty or thirty years of their long lives - John and Nessie, Charles and Arabella - side by side in Parkgate Road.

Recognition

After decades of disappointment and rejection, John Monk and other ageing officers of his generation began, belatedly, to receive some of the recognition they felt their naval service deserved, although it took intervention by the young Queen

Victoria to bring it about.

Before 1816, medals had generally been awarded only to senior officers who had led campaigns or won battles. After the Battle of Waterloo, however, with the vigorous support of the Duke of Wellington, a campaign medal was awarded to every officer and soldier who had taken part. In contrast, nothing was awarded to the men who had fought at the many other campaigns during this period. This apparent lack of appreciation led to resentment among former soldiers and seamen, a feeling that remained despite the passing years.

Requests were made for these veterans to be honoured, but the Duke of Wellington this time argued against it. Momentum grew in 1845 when the veteran Duke of Richmond presented a petition in the House of Lords urging that junior officers, non-commissioned officers and men should receive recognition of their services during the long conflict. The petition was initially rejected, until Queen Victoria overruled the decision. In June 1847, she announced that a medal would be issued retrospectively to officers and men of the Royal Navy, to commemorate various naval actions during the French Revolutionary Wars, the Napoleonic Wars and a handful of later actions.

The Naval General Service Medal and its military equivalent were finally issued in June 1849, by which time many who had fought were no longer alive. Clasps were authorised for 231 battles and actions, from boat service and ship-to-ship skirmishes, to major fleet actions such as the Battle of Trafalgar. The medal was silver, with Queen Victoria on one side and the figure of Britannia on the other, holding a trident and seated on a seahorse. It was available to surviving claimants only, fifty-six years after the first event and more than thirty years since peace with France. Instructions for claiming the medal required veterans to apply to Whitehall and provide evidence of their involvement.

Back in Neston, John and George Louthean prepared forms A and B as required, but still needed to support John's application with a testimonial. All his old commanders were long since dead, so John contacted Francis Brace, nephew of Edward Brace and formerly a fellow officer on the *Berwick*. John felt Francis owed him a favour, having once fired on him accidentally in the heat of battle as John led a captured French schooner out of Negaye harbour.[21]

John's application was approved, and in 1850 he received his medal with its two clasps, one for the relentless nights of boat service during the assault on Gaeta in 1815 and another for the bloody bombardment of Algiers a year later.

As well as the issuing of the Naval General Service Medal, 1849 was noteworthy for another reason in John's pursuit of recognition. It marked the publication of the *Naval Biographical Dictionary* by William O'Byrne, full title *A Naval Biographical Dictionary: Comprising the Life and Services of Every Living Officer in Her Majesty's Navy, from the Rank of Admiral of the Fleet to that of Lieutenant, Inclusive*. This mammoth volume brought together biographical notes and details of naval careers for every officer of the Royal Navy alive in 1845, almost five thousand officers, listed alphabetically by surname. O'Byrne compiled his book using both official records and personal submissions from the officers themselves. Contributions were requested from every officer concerned and then cross-referenced against the London Gazette.[22] It was a huge undertaking, which took six years to prepare and ran to over 1,400 pages. Today, though, for many officers, the descriptions of their service contained in O'Byrne's great work are the clearest record that remains. And there, on page 771, between *George Mitford Monk* and *Edward Proudfoot Montagu* is *John Monk, (Lieutenant, 1814)*, with a column to himself.

The rank of commander to which John had aspired earlier in his career had at first presented a stepping stone to captain and the progression to rear-admiral beyond that, but it had been many long years since he had last seen active service. The Admiralty's general intention in placing commissioned officers on half-pay was to ensure that enough men could be called to arms in the event of war, but an officer's commission was an appointment for life, with no specified retirement age, which gave the Admiralty a problem. With each passing year away from active service, an officer on half-pay was increasingly unlikely to find himself called to serve again in any capacity. The Navy List had become clogged with elderly officers like John.

On April 13th, 1857, the Admiralty offered John a promotion, but with strings attached, as it came with an acceptance that it would mark his retirement. An earlier letter from John during his campaign for promotion shows that he was increasingly resigned to this, and, at the age of 66, accepting may not have been too difficult a decision. John was promoted to Commander (Superannuated) and indicated as such on the Navy List. His promotion had come too late to help his career, and the hunt for recognition had caused him years of frustration, but John's long-running battle with the Admiralty was finally at an end.

A couple of years later, John had the perfect reason to don his uniform once more, attach his medal and to resume his position as naval officer, albeit ceremonially. War had broken out in April 1859 between France and the Austrian Empire, and there were fears that Britain might be caught up in a wider European conflict or face invasion by the French. To help defend its shores, the British government authorised the formation of local volunteer rifle corps.

Judge Horatio Lloyd chaired a committee of local landowners and prominent citizens, among them the vicar and the town doctor, David Russell, who together created the 11th Cheshire (Neston) Rifle Volunteers. Military credibility was lent by the involvement of local ex-servicemen, including Commander John Monk for the Navy. John and brother Charles each donated £10 and were made honorary members.[23]

Participation in formal dinners and toasting ceremonies were an important part of the role of an honorary member. One such occasion was described by the *Liverpool Daily Post*. The Volunteers mustered one Friday in January 1861, to be drilled and inspected, and were then marched to the new school building in Liverpool Road, where they sat down for dinner with John and other honorary members. The ceremony and formal rules governing the dinner would have been familiar from John's days of active service in the Royal Navy forty years earlier, when Captain Brace would have led similar toasts with his officers in his cabin aboard the *Berwick*. A toast was proposed by the chair to 'The Army and Navy', which Commander Monk and a Captain Torrens duly acknowledged, as tradition dictated.[24]

The most prominent memorial to John Monk's life can be found just off Neston High Street, inside his local church of St Mary and St Helen. In 1874, six years before his death, an elderly John gifted the church £120 (about £7,500 today) to pay for the design and construction of one of the large stained-glass windows which were added during its rebuilding.[25]

Work on the church had become necessary after a century of ill-advised modifications, often on the insistence of wealthy parishioners, had left the structure unstable to the point where a near-complete rebuild was required. The last of these had been a fourth raised gallery added in 1772, and this time John's grandfather John Matthews had been among those demanding it. When the work was completed, though, the families had complained that a structural pillar now blocked their view of the pulpit. To get around this problem, the pillar was simply removed and a wider arch added in its place.

The Monk window, as it is known, stands to the left of the entrance to the rebuilt church, beside the ancient font in which John had been baptized as an infant in 1791, and in which a blacksmith's daughter called Amy Lyon had also been baptized a quarter of a century earlier, most famously remembered today as Lady Hamilton, Nelson's mistress and muse to the artist George Romney.

It is an indication of the regard in which John was held within the community, but also perhaps of his own character, that there is so much of him in the window. Each of the three tall narrow scenes depicts a biblical story of the sea from the New Testament. In the window reveals, large brass plates commemorate John, his siblings and each of his Parkgate ancestors, right back to his great-great-grandfather, Samuel Matthews, born in 1641. Many of these ancestors are buried just feet away in the Matthews family's plot in the church graveyard, immediately outside the church door, although the stones lie flat and are now largely illegible. The window strikes an interesting balance. The subject matter is biblical and worshipful, but arguably the effect is to commemorate the Monk and Matthews families.

The reopening of the church and the unveiling of the Monk window in November 1875 came at a time of change for John. He was 84, still being described as 'hale and hearty' in a letter that year to the *Wrexham Guardian*,[26] but within a year or two he would begin a slow slide into senility. His brother Charles had died aged 92 in January 1874, the cause of death recorded as 'natural decay'. Nessie had died of liver disease in December the same year, and Arabella had followed in September 1875. Ann began a mental decline around this time and would die in Chester in December 1879, after which only John remained.

As the end approached, John may have felt a shimmer of sadness and satisfaction as he looked up at the brass name plates which surrounded the pictures in the coloured glass, realising that this window would keep their memories alive.

Decline

John's eventual decline was seemingly precipitated by a fall on the ice, after which he grew steadily more confused and eccentric in his behaviour.[27] His sister Ann's son, William Brown,

211

took an increasingly active role in his uncle's care during these final years. In December 1876, perhaps worried about him being alone since Nessie's death, William arranged for John, recently turned 85, to move closer to him in Chester and set him up briefly in a Grosvenor Street lodging house. In May of the following year, William found himself involved in an unusual court case, which centred on the size of his aged uncle's appetite.

John remained at his Grosvenor Street lodgings until March 1877, when William paid the proprietor, Thomas Rowland, £2 by way of a week's notice. Rowland claimed he had already spent money on provisions for the week ahead and demanded an additional £1, which William refused to pay. At Chester county court, Judge Horatio Lloyd asked whether so much had really been spent, to which Rowland replied that John's table was 'most liberally supplied; he had five courses each day'. Unfortunately for Rowland, the judge knew John personally from his involvement with the Cheshire Volunteers and recalled that 'he used to be a man of simple habits, and didn't use to have many courses', adding doubtfully that it was 'astonishing that an old gentleman of 86 could eat so much as represented'. Rowland pleaded 'Yes, but Mr Brown knows he is as hearty as a bullock!' This caused laughter in the courtroom, but Rowland's claim was still dismissed.[28] After this brief sojourn in Chester, John returned to Parkgate Road, under the constant watch of a full-time carer, John Warden, who saw John's mental state deteriorate.

It is hard to know what to make of the eventual violence of John's demise. He had known death in all its guises throughout his lifetime, whether it was among the bloody carnage of Algiers, the premature mourning of countless young nephews and nieces lost to tuberculosis, or the gradual decay of his brothers and sisters as old age took its toll. As John's confusion and likely dementia worsened, his thoughts became increasingly dark. At the inquest which followed John's death, Warden would report that, in the preceding two years, John had frequently threatened to strangle himself or take his life in some other way, and on one occasion he had even asked Warden to give him some poison. Warden testified that John had made these threats so often that, after a while, those close to him took little notice.

The morning of Sunday, May 2nd, 1880, began as most Sundays did. Warden left the house, as usual, to go to the ten a.m. church service. As he did whenever he went out, he left John in the care of Mary, the housekeeper. On this particular morning, the house had been quiet for about ten minutes when John came downstairs and told Mary that he intended to 'be quiet for a bit'. Mary agreed not to disturb him, and John went back upstairs to his bedroom.

After several minutes of silence, Mary's attention was attracted first by a thud and then a groaning noise from above. Heading upstairs, she found John hanging from a bedpost by a silk handkerchief. Mary tried desperately to lift him back on to the bed before she found a knife and cut him down. She hurried outside and sent for Dr Russell, who was a neighbour at Vine House and had been John's physician for many years. When the doctor arrived, he found John still alive, although barely, and attempted to resuscitate him. After more than half an hour of fruitless efforts, together with Mary and John

Warden, who had been called back from the church, Dr Russell pronounced John dead.

In the days that followed, John Monk's passing was reported in newspapers in several counties, such as the following from the *Liverpool Echo*:

He was very well known in the district of Parkgate and Neston, where he and other members his family had long resided. In his younger days, he had seen a good deal of active service in the navy. He used to take great delight at times in recounting the stirring adventures through which he had passed.[29]

Deaths by suicide were a popular topic in Victorian newspapers. Articles would give a nod to the 'sad demise', but revelled unashamedly in the events, recounting every gruesome detail. In their report of John's death, the *Crewe Chronicle* delightedly described, 'his tongue protruding from his mouth, and his face black from suffocation'.[30]

An inquest was held the following day at the Golden Lion Inn on the High Street, where coroner Henry Churton returned a verdict of 'Committed suicide whilst in a state of unsound mind.'[31] Accounts of John's final years leave no doubt as to his mental decline, although suicide verdicts were commonly worded in this way. It was done, in a sense, to protect the memory or reputation of the deceased, as it was technically a criminal act to take one's life while of a sound mind, right up until 1961.

John's estate became a source of speculation in the days after his death. The *Liverpool Echo* reported that, 'the deceased leaves behind him a large amount of wealth, which, he never having been married, goes to some nephews residing in Chester', adding with regards to Charles: 'A brother of the deceased gentleman died some little time ago, it is said, the age of ninety-five, leaving property to the amount of about half a million.'[32]

John's will was proved on May 21st, 1880, and his estate was assessed at under £8,000, roughly £500,000 in today's money. As the *Liverpool Echo* had predicted, the greater part did indeed go to nephews William and Charles Brown, who acted as executors, but a large share went also to his niece Nessie Moore, younger daughter of John's brother Whitehouse.[33]

There were several charitable bequests worthy of note. On her death in 1875, John's sister Nessie Matthews had left £100 for the benefit of the poor, to be administered by her nephew, William Brown. Now, in 1880, John left a further £200 for the same purpose. William combined the funds and formed what became known as the Matthews and Monk Charity. In the years that followed, the charity regularly distributed food, clothing, and blankets to the poor in the Neston and Parkgate area. It was registered by the Charity Commission in 1915, 'for the benefit of the poor and needy of the parish of Neston generally'. Unusually, the Matthews and Monk Charity remains active today, despite the original funds being depleted over time. Through local fundraising events and donations, it continues to distribute Christmas gifts and gives help towards studies and apprenticeships.[34]

John also left £500 to the Royal National Lifeboat Institute, an organisation close to every sailor's heart. His bequest came with exacting demands as to how the funds were to be used:

I bequeath the following charitable legacies free from legacy duty, namely to the Royal Lifeboat Institution the sum of five hundred pounds for the purpose and on the condition of that Institution building a Life Boat which shall be named 'The John Monk'.[35]

The insistence that the lifeboat must be named after him was by no means standard practice. It was common for a lifeboat station to name a boat after a benefactor, but for it to be a condition of the bequest was distinctly less so. As dutiful executors, William and Charles made enquiries with the Dock Board and found that a boat meeting John's requirements could not be placed on the Lancashire, Cheshire or Welsh coasts. Undeterred, they looked further afield for alternatives. William knew the Isle of Man well, and had close friends in the fishing port of Peel on the west coast. William's application to the Manx authorities was accepted, and the *John Monk* lifeboat, a brand new thirty-seven foot, twelve-oared self-righter, was placed in the Peel lifeboat station in 1885.[36]

William had chosen well. Located towards the north of the Irish Sea, the Isle of Man had been a silent witness to much of John's long, eventful life. The island's rocky southern shore had stood close by through the years, as John guided his brig home from Leghorn to Liverpool, as he battled his way southwards through the storm of 1824, or as he travelled from Neston to Sandymount to visit the sisters he held so dear. The title of this book promised an account of a life in the Royal Navy and merchant service, but by the time of John's death, he had lived quietly among friends and family for far longer than his more dramatic years at sea. The focus of a younger man on career and fortune had mellowed into a quieter dedication to family and community.

Grander and more public lives have certainly been led, but, as the Neston church officer prepared to memorialise John's years in brass and as William sought to honour his wish that a lifeboat should bear his name, John could hopefully have looked back upon a life well lived or, at least, a battle well fought.

Epilogue. The Irish Sea, October 7th, 1889

The storm in the Irish Sea continued to rage as the crew of volunteers, under command of the coxswain, Charley Cain, rowed the *John Monk* towards the stricken ship, constantly bailing as powerful waves threatened to overwhelm their little boat.

The vessel that the crew of the Peel lifeboat were attempting to reach was the Norwegian cargo ship *St George*, which had left Greenock on Saturday night bound for Monte Video. On board the stricken ship, Captain Thorensen had accepted that all was lost, and that he, his wife and young baby and the crew of twenty would all die. They had survived the night somehow but he knew that their prospects were bleak. A crew member later recalled how he asked Thorensen whether they should be making rafts and got the reply, 'Do what you like. We shall have to go down, and there is nothing to do.'[1]

Drawing close to the Norwegian ship, after three hours of rowing and bailing, the Peel lifeboatmen could see that she was a complete wreck and would be impossible to approach. She had lost her masts, and floating all around her were tangles of rope, sails and spars. A man on board waved a flag to get their attention, and shouted across the debris that there were twenty-three on board. With no way to get closer, the lifeboat crew heaved a buoy out towards the ship and began to pull each person in through the water, one at a time, while eight of the crew manned the oars to hold their position. The captain's wife came first, next the carpenter carrying her nine-month-old baby tied up in a canvas bag and slung between his shoulders, and then the rest of the Norwegian ship's company. The poor ship's dog was left to meet his maker on the sinking ship.

With her additional twenty-three passengers squeezed on board, the *John Monk* headed home. The boat sat low in the water as the oarsmen rowed back towards the shore. The wind was behind them, now speeding them homewards, although a large wave risked swamping the stern at any point. The lifeboat-men and their passengers finally reached the harbour, where they were met by a cheering crowd of thousands. Someone in the crowd immediately took the baby to find a warm fire and dry clothing, a kind act which unfortunately left the desperate captain's wife searching for her baby all over the town.[2] What remained of the *St. George* was wrecked on the rocks by Peel Castle that night, leaving the beach strewn with debris.

In the months after the rescue, the *John Monk* lifeboat and her crew became a source of pride on the island, and the subject of songs and poems. The coxswain even received a medal from the King of Norway.

The old wooden lifeboat was replaced long ago, but the rescue of the *St George* on October 7th, 1889, was not forgotten. The crew of the *John Monk* are still honoured by a plaque in the Peel lifeboat station, together with the figurehead of the *St George*, salvaged from the rocky beach in the days after the storm.

The centenary of the rescue came in 1989. The Isle of Man issued a commemorative postal cover, and a service of thanks-giving was held at Peel Cathedral to mark the occasion. More than 180 years had passed since a young John had first set foot on HMS *Dictator*, but every life will send its ripples into the future. One of the guests at the festivities in Peel was a Norwegian lady called Karin, the daughter of Sigrid, the baby who been rescued by the lifeboat crew all those years before.

John would have been delighted.

In connection with the recent lifeboat service at Peel, by which 23 lives were saved from the wreck of the St. George, last week, the following letter has been received: –

Sir,.– Allow me, as one to whom Peel and its belongings are doubly dear, to congratulate you and your fellow-men who have just gained such a noble victory... You have, all of you, shown yourselves brave men, and I for one, am very proud of you all... –

I am, sir, respectfully yours, FLORENCE DUDLEY

THE "JOHN MONK" CREW!

Speak not of deeds in battles wrought
By men whose brain has fully thought
Out all the plans for victory's fame
To give themselves a hero's name ;
Far nobler those brave men who tried
To reach the drifting vessel's side.
Who gave up thought of life and friends
To gain sweet mercy's nobler ends!
Then with good voices raise anew
This cheer, "God bless the John Monk crew."

Long may our God the lives prolong
Of these brave men, whose will so strong
Braved sea and storm - stern perils dared
God helped them on; all lives were spared :
And every wave that touched the strand
Helped on the boat so bravely manned ;
Whilst Malin Creg and Peel Hill side
The cheers re-echoed far and wide.
And distant voices raise anew
This cheer, "God bless the John Monk crew."

Acknowledgements

Telling John's tale has only been possible because of the kind and generous support offered by so many people along the way. I have done my best here to thank everyone involved, but sincere apologies to anyone I have missed. I am grateful to all of the following for their input, corrections and comments. Any remaining mistakes are strictly my own.

Martyn Beardsley, for his editorial direction, and for helping me meet my subject. Stella Young and Geoff Wright, for friendship and helping to place John and his siblings properly in the Neston and Parkgate community. Authors Margaret Muir and Linda Collison for so much mentoring, expertise and encouragement. James Essinger and the team at The Conrad Press, and Charlotte Mouncey at Bookstyle. Len Barnett, for lending his many years of nautical expertise. Giuseppe 'Pippo' Moccaldi, who researched John's Italian connection to the Massone family. Rosemary Mead, for enjoyable dinners and for very kindly providing access to family papers. Further knowledge and insights were generously provided by Susan Taylor, Susan Chambers, Anthony Annakin-Smith and Sheryl Hazelgrove, and my thanks also to Louise Benson, for research of the Grosvenor Estate archive, and Janice Quilliam, ancestor the wonderfully named William Quilliam who manned the Peel lifeboat on the day of the St George rescue.

This biography has been enriched by a wealth of personal letters and anecdotes carefully collected and passed through the years, with each generation adding what they can. This work would not have been possible without the efforts through the generations of William Brown, Harry Faulkner Brown, and Stephen Humfrey Brown.

And thanks also to family and friends who reviewed drafts along the way, among them my mother, Anne Brown, my brother Julian, and Tony Shipley, Elizabeth Brooks, Jason Cooke and Brett Dolman. And a very special thanks to my wife Karine and children, Emma, Ben and Tara, mainly for their patience!

Appendix: Untellable tales

When researching the life of someone who lived more than two hundred years ago, there will always be stories that stubbornly remain in the shadows. This is particularly true for a man like John Monk, a keen storyteller, happy to weave the fabric of his life from hard facts and loose retellings. John's obituary in the *Chester Chronicle* gives us a tantalising glimpse of an episode which it is difficult to verify:

On his discharge on half-pay in 1816, he joined the Italian patriots and fought under Charles Albert in the war of Independence.[1]

Prince Charles Albert was to become an important figure in Italian unification, but in his younger years he would not have had any need for a naval officer's services. He had been educated in France during the Napoleonic years, and when he returned to Italy his liberal views were at odds with the absolute monarchy of which he was part. He gave, and then withdrew, support for a rebellion seeking a constitutional monarchy in 1821, and then left the country until 1824 when he had been forgiven for his previous liberal ideas.

It is possible of course that William was simply mixing up the names. An alternative would be Victor Emmanuel I, the King of Sardinia from 1802 to 1821. He had spent several days on John's ship the *Berwick* while in Genoa in August 1815. However, he was decidedly conservative and unwound many of the progressive changes introduced under Napoleon's reign. His agenda was firmly domestic and his need for a foreign naval officer would have been similarly limited.

If John had any involvement with the Sardinian royal family, it was most likely with Charles Felix, who ascended to the throne after his brother's abdication in 1821. His official residence was in Turin, but he generally spent little time there outside of the theatre season and preferred his home in Genoa. John may have been introduced to him or members of his court through the Massone family, who were influential in the area.

In 1825, Sardinia became involved in a short war with Tripoli where John's experiences in the spring of 1816 may have been of use. The Dey of Tripoli was offended by Sardinia's refusal to pay increased tribute and declared war. In response, Charles Felix sent ships to Tripoli to reinforce the agreements reached during Pellew's diplomatic visit of 1816. John may have been of help to Charles Felix in planning this conflict, but at the time of the battle itself, on September 26th, 1825, he was on the *William Black*, en route from Leghorn to Dublin.

There is one other factor which calls William's account into question and means this episode is perhaps best filed under Untellable Tales. The Admiralty was generally willing to grant leave of absence to officers, but with certain expectations. For John to have served a 'Foreign Prince or State' would have required him to resign his naval commission, with the loss of both his status as an officer and the security of a lieutenant's half-pay. The story of John's life shows that he would have been very reluctant to relinquish either one of these.

Endnotes

Prologue

[1] Account based on booklet 'The Wreck of the St. George', (1989, *Peel City Guardian*) and *Isle of Man Times,* Wednesday 09 October 1889

1. A childhood in Parkgate

[1] Paston. *Mrs. Delany (Mary Granville) : a memoir, 1700-1788* (Grant Richards, 1900)

[2] JM.07.04. Certificate appointing William Monk to landwaiter in the port of Chester, 1775

[3] Captain Peter Hore, *Nelson's Band of Brothers: Lives and Memorials* (Seaforth, 2015)

2. Volunteer, first-class

[1] JM.02.11. Active Service summaries (x4)

[2] Lavery. *The Ship of the Line, Volume 1* (Conway Maritime Press, 2003)

[3] The 'ship of the line' term refers to the typical battle formation, in which these gun-heavy ships would traditionally follow each other bow-to-stern in column formation before exchanging broadsides with the enemy.

[4] The National Archives (TNA): ADM 51/1630

[5] Paul F. State, *A Brief History of the Netherlands* (2008)

[6] TNA: HCA 32/1707/6118

[7] From marriage licence, 1802

[8] Details of Macnamara's family including his portrait are based on Nottidge Charles MacNamara, *The Story of an Irish Sept* (J.M. Dent, 1896)

[9] Andrew Steinmetz, *The Romance of Duelling in All Times and Countries*, Vol. 2, (1868), p186

[10] J.S. Clarke, John McArthur (ed), *The Naval Chronicle*: Volume 9, January-July 1803

[11] Nottidge Charles MacNamara, *The Story of an Irish Sept* (J.M. Dent,

1896)

[12] TNA: ADM 1/2153, ADM 1/2154, ADM 1/2155, ADM 1/2156 (Letters from Captains, Surnames M: 1807)

[13] Based on Wendy Hinde, *George Canning* (1973) p169

[14] William James, *The Naval History of Great Britain*, Volume III, 1805-1807, (Richard Bentley, 1837), p421

[15] Account based on Richard Cavendish, 'The Bombardment of Copenhagen' (*History Today*, Volume 57 Issue 9, September 2007), and Thomas Munch-Petersen, *Defying Napoleon: How Britain Bombarded Copenhagen and Seized the Danish Fleet in 1807* (Sutton, 2007)

[16] JM.02.13, Letter received with notes on active service, 1840, and JM.02.11. Active Service Summary

[17] Tim Voelcker, *Admiral Saumarez Versus Napoleon: The Baltic, 1807-12*, (Boydell Press, 2008) p16

3. Baltic ice

[1] JM.02.01. Letter to Richard Grosvenor

[2] TNA: ADM 1/2157, ADM 1/2158, ADM 1/2159 (Letters from Captains, Surnames M: 1808)

[3] TNA: ADM 1/5386 (Courts Martial Papers)

[4] TNA: ADM 1/5386 (Courts Martial Papers)

[5] TNA: PRIS 11/16 (Entry book of Admiralty prisoners, 1800-1823)

[6] TNA: ADM 1/2157, ADM 1/2158, ADM 1/2159 (Letters from Captains, Surnames M: 1808)

[7] Rod Dickson, *Maritime Heritage Association journal*, Volume 22, No. 3. September 2011 'Royal Navy Punishments'

[8] TNA: ADM 51/2336 (Captains' logs, including: EDGAR (1808 July 1-1810 Dec 8))

[9] This account is based on Charles Oman, *A History of the Peninsula War*, Vol. 1, 1807-1809 (Clarendon Press, 1902), and Hon. Sir Edward Cust, *Annals of the wars of the nineteenth century*. Vol. 2, 1807-1809 (John Murray, 1862), p120

[10] JM.02.13, Letter received with notes on active service, 1840, and JM.02.11. Active Service Summary

[11] TNA: ADM 1/2157, ADM 1/2158, ADM 1/2159 (Letters from Captains, Surnames M: 1808)

[12] JM.02.13, Letter received with notes on active service, 1840, and

JM.02.11. Active Service Summary

[13] TNA: ADM 53/462 (Ships' Logs)

[14] TNA: ADM 1/2160, ADM 1/2161 (Letters from Captains, Surnames M: 1809)

[15] TNA: ADM 51/2336 (Captains' logs, including: EDGAR (1808 July 1-1810 Dec 8))

[16] TNA: ADM 51/2336 (Captains' logs, including: EDGAR (1808 July 1-1810 Dec 8))

[17] TNA: HCA 32/1035/2372

[18] William Stephen Gilly, *Narratives of Shipwrecks of the Royal Navy; Between 1793 and 1849* (1850)

[19] JM.07.06. Letter to Edward Acton Gibbon from Solomon Boileau

[20] Place, *The Rise and Fall of Parkgate*, p257

[21] 'William Monk of Parkgate', by portraitist Albin R Burt, 1819

[22] *Manchester Courier and Lancashire General Advertiser*, 01 October 1842: "Parkgate is noted for a swearing people; and in the evenings the young lads lounge about on the terrace walls, and insult the passers-by; but a good thrashing from two or three of the gentlemen promenaders would do them the world of good."

[23] Based on Place, *The Rise and Fall of Parkgate*, p257, and 'Wrecks in the Dee Estuary', Chris Michael (University of Liverpool website).

[24] M. Rowe, *Collaboration and Resistance in Napoleonic Europe* (Palgrave Macmillan, 2003), p210

[25] *Bury and Norwich Post*, 28 March 1810

[26] TNA: HCA 32/1045/2598

4. South to warmer seas

[1] J.J. Colledge, Ben Warlow, *Ships of the Royal Navy* (Chatham, 2010), p44

[2] TNA: ADM 1/2162, ADM 1/2163, ADM 1/2164 (Letters from Captains, Surnames M; 1810)

[3] TNA: ADM 51/2149 (Captains' logs, including: BERWICK (1810 Mar 17-1813 Dec 31))

[4] Andrew D. Lambert, *The Last Sailing Battlefleet*, (Conway Maritime, 1991) p68

[5] TNA: ADM 51/2149 (Captains' logs, including: BERWICK (1810 Mar 17-1813 Dec 31))

6   Robert Feuardent, *La perte de la frégate 'L'Amazone', Mémoires de la Société nationale académique de Cherbourg*, vol. 28, 1975

7   Nicholas Tracy, *Who's Who in Nelson's Navy*. p236.

8   John Knox Laughton, *Dictionary of National Biography*, 1885-1900, Volume 35, 'James Macnamara'

9   TNA: ADM 1/5431 (Courts Martial Papers)

10   JM.02.13. Letter to Self.

11   Account based on Edward Brace's letter in *The London Gazette*, From Saturday, July 3 to Tuesday, July 6, 1813, p1

12   TNA: ADM 51/2149 (Captains' logs, including: BERWICK (1810 Mar 17-1813 Dec 31))

13   *The London Gazette*, From Saturday, July 3 to Tuesday, July 6, 1813

14   JM.02.01. Letter to Richard Grosvenor

15   TNA: HCA 32/1323/1938

16   TNA: HCA 32/1330/2057 & HCA 32/1330/2058

17   *Naval Biographical Dictionary*, William O'Byrne. John Murray, 1849.

18   JM.02.11.1 Active Service Summary

19   William O'Byrne, full title *A Naval Biographical Dictionary: Comprising the Life and Services of Every Living Officer in Her Majesty's Navy, from the Rank of Admiral of the Fleet to that of Lieutenant, Inclusive.* John Murray, 1849.

20   JM.02.13, Letter received with notes on active service, 1840

21   JM.02.08 Letter to Geo Louthean, 1848

22   O. Troude, *Batailles navales de la France, Volume 4*, (2010)

23   JM.02.11. Active Service summaries (x4)

24   Bob Burnham, Ron McGuigan, *The British Army Against Napoleon: Facts, Lists and Trivia, 1805-1815* (Frontline, 2010 p52)

25   TNA: ADM 53/159

26   Based on David Nicholls, *Napoleon: A Biographical Companion* (1999) p1, and Encyclopaedia Britannica website, 'Treaties of Paris 1814-1815'

27   JM.04.01. Letter from Nessie Brown to William Brown, 23 May 1881

28   JM.02.01. Letter to Richard Grosvenor

29   JM.04.02. Letter from Eleanora and Teresa Massone. 20 Aug 1814

30   JM.04.15. Letter from Marcello Massone. 10 Feb 1817

31   JM.04.04. Letter from Teresa Massone. Undated.

32   JM.02.01. Letter to Richard Grosvenor

33   David Nicholls, *Napoleon: A Biographical Companion* (1999) p28

34   Caiani. *To Kidnap a Pope: Napoleon and Pius VII* (Yale, 2021)

35   *The Naval Chronicle, Volume 34.* Letter from Wm Charles Fahie to Lord Exmouth, 23 July 1815, p344

36   *The Naval Chronicle, Volume 34.* Letter from Wm Charles Fahie to Lord Exmouth, 23 July 1815, p344

37   JM.04.07 Letter from Teresa. Genoa the 19th of July 1815

38   JM.04.17. Letter from Marcello Massone. 18 Jun 1817

5. Algiers and the *Impregnable*

1   JM.02.01. Letter to Richard Grosvenor.

2   *The Popular Encyclopedia: Or, Conversations Lexicon, Volume 6,* (Blackie & Son, 1862) p285

3   Stephen Taylor gives a vibrant and detailed account of Pellew's diplomatic mission and his return to Algiers, in *Commander*, his excellent biography of Edward Pellew, to which this account is indebted.

4   Letter from Lord Exmouth to the Dey of Algiers, August 28th, 1816. Quoted in Sir Frederick Thomas Michell, P*ersonal recollections of the expedition to Algiers in August*, 1816, (1865) p73

5   John Marshall, *Royal Naval Biography*, (1824, Longman) p260

6   JM.02.11. Active service summaries (x4)

7   Stephen Taylor, *Commander* (Faber & Faber, 2012) p266

8   Quoted from ThreeDecks.org, 2014. 'Letter from a Midshipman, of the Impregnable, Admiral Milne's ship, His Majesty's ship Impregnable, Algiers Bay, Aug. 29, 1816'

9   William James, *The Naval History of Great Britain, Vol VI* (Harding, Lepard, and Co., 1826) p577

10   Published in *Chester Courant*, 01 October 1816

11   JM.02.11. Active Service summary

12   Perkins & Douglas-Morris. *Gunfire in Barbary.* Mason, 1982. p151

13   Published in *Chester Courant*, 1 October 1816

14   Micheal Clodfelter, *Warfare and Armed Conflicts: A Statistical Encyclopedia* (2017), p198

15   William James, *The Naval History of Great Britain, Vol VI* (Bentley, 1837) p409

16   John Marshall, *Royal Naval Biography*, (1824, Longman) p260

17   *Naval & Military Gazette*, 3 September 1879

18 *Naval & Military Gazette and Weekly Chronicle of the United Service,* 06 October 1875

19 KP Hunter & RJ Rogers, *HMS Caledonia - the Royal Naval Engineering School - a short history.*

20 JM.04.13. Letter from Marcello Massone. 15 Sep 1816

21 Place, *The Rise and Fall of Parkgate,* p258

22 *Chester Courant,* 02 October 1821

23 Martin Wilcox. 'These Peaceable Times are the Devil: Royal Navy Officers in the Post-War Slump, 1815-1825', 2014. *International Journal of Maritime History.*

24 Martin Wilcox. 'These Peaceable Times are the Devil: Royal Navy Officers in the Post-War Slump, 1815-1825', 2014. *International Journal of Maritime History.*

25 Robert Southey, *The Life of Nelson* (1878), George Routledge

26 *Chester Courant,* 01 June 1819

27 JM.07.07.Letter from Joseph Monk to sister Esther (Nessie) Matthews. 1826

28 JM.07.07.Letter from Joseph Monk to sister Esther (Nessie) Matthews. 1826

29 Transcript of letters of admission to the Asylum (dated 9th February 1836):
'I hereby certify that I have examined carefully Mr Whitehouse Monk of Neston and find him of unsound mind and a fit person to be placed in an asylum for medical treatment.
(signed) J. W. Bankes, J. Mitchell
We the undersigned being assured as well from our own observation as by the annexed medical certificate that Mr Whitehouse Monk is of unsound mind do hereby request you to receive him into the Chester Asylum. (signed) Charles Monk, Henry Smith'
Source: Cheshire Record Office, Chester

30 JM.03.01. Letter from Catisfield (Edward Brace). 8 Nov 1817

31 TNA: ADM 1/1562, ADM 1/1563. Letters from Captains, Surnames B: 1816

32 morethannelson.com website profile of Sir Edward Brace (last visited 1/9/2022)

33 *Chester Chronicle,* 1 September 1815

34 A good write-up of the English election system at this time appears in

David Cordingly's book, *Cochrane the Dauntless,* about his subject's venture into politics.

[35] JM.05.01. Note from General (Thomas) Grosvenor. 13 Mar 1820

[36] *Poll Book for the General Election...* 1820, J. Fletcher, Chester, pp 19&30

[37] *Chester Courant,* 21 August 1821 and 22 July 1823

[38] JM.04.15. Letter from Marcello Massone. 10 Feb 1817

[39] TNA: ADM 1/3034

[40] Martin Wilcox. 'These Peaceable Times are the Devil: Royal Navy Officers in the Post-War Slump, 1815-1825', 2014. *International Journal of Maritime History.*

[41] *Isle of Man Times,* 9 November 1889

[42] *Trial of Charles Christopher Delano and Others,* London, John Murray, 1820. Also, 'Pirates in the Early British Era: The Malta Connections', Giovanni Bonello (The Malta Historical Society, 2010)

[43] Andrew Bigelow, *Travels in Malta and Sicily,* (1831), p172

[44] The author William H.G. Kingston used Delano's story almost unchanged in his adventure novel Salt Water (1865)

[45] JM.04.20. Letter from Marco Massone. 15 May 1822

[46] JM.04.20. Letter from Marco Massone. 15 May 1822

6. A voyage on the *William Black*

[1] TNA: ADM 1/3035

[2] *Chester Chronicle,* 15 July 1825

[3] TNA: ADM 1/3036

[4] Wikipedia. Derived from 'List of shipwrecks in 1824'. Last accessed 17 Aug 2020.

[5] JM.06.03. Diary of Journey, Italy (booklet). 1824

[6] Probable initials (not clearly decipherable in the manuscript).

[7] Whether this figure of £75,000 reflects John's assets or was plucked from the air for dramatic effect is unknown, but following his death in 1880, his estate was valued at "Under £8,000".

[8] *Chester Courant,* 24 August 1824

[9] *P.Q., St James's Park: A Comedy,* (1733), p58

[10] *The General Lover, Or Small Talker, a Series of Letters from a Lady in the West of England to Lady Anne D-, Abroad* (full title), Anonymous (1769)

11 *Songs, chorusses, &c. in The campaign; or, love in the East-Indies. A comic opera.* Captain Robert Jephson (1803)

12 Mons Abyla. Modern day Ceuta, the Spanish autonomous city on the African coast.

13 Kevin Brown, *The Seasick Admiral: Nelson and the Health of the Navy* (Seaforth, 2015)

14 Fergus Fleming, *The Sword and the Cross* (Granta, 2007)

15 *Bath Chronicle and Weekly Gazette*, 23 December 1824

16 Probable initials (not clearly decipherable in the manuscript)

17 Based on The Dawlish Chronicles website article, 'The Loss of the East Indiaman Kent', and Anthony Brandt, The Tragic History of the Sea, (National Geographic, 2007)

18 *Chester Chronicle*, 09 January 1829

19 *Chester Courant*, 13 February 1827

20 *Gore's Liverpool General Advertiser*, 29 November 1827

21 JM.05.05. Letter to Richard Grosvenor (undated copy). Maraskins is known today as maraschino, a cherry-flavoured liqueur.

22 *Liverpool Mercury*, 30 August 1833, p7 (quantity abbreviations spelt out here in full)

23 Henry Mayhew, *London Labour and the London Poor*, 1851

24 There were other emporia and warehouses in Leghorn at the time, but Micali's, established in 1760, was renowned for offering a wide range of goods, including Ancient Egyptian pieces, English prints, Wedgwood creamware, embroidered Chinese silk, jewellery, porcelain, crystal, as well as marble and alabaster sculptures.

25 JM.06.03. Diary of Journey. Italy (booklet). 1824

26 *Cheshire Observer*, 16 May 1877

27 Will from General Records Office. Probate 21 May 1880. Folio 274

28 Based on Charles Pope, *The Merchant, Ship-Owner, and Ship-Master's Import and Export Guide* (1831), and John Booker, *Maritime Quarantine: The British Experience*, c.1650–1900 (2007)

29 *Lloyd's Register (Underwriters)*, 1827

30 *Dublin Mercantile Advertiser*, 22 December 1828

31 *Lloyds Register*, 1833-1834

7. The *Monk*

1   JM.07.07.Letter from Joseph Monk to sister Esther (Nessie) Matthews. 1826

2   TNA: PROB 11/2099/401

3   Based on accounts in the *Chester Courant*, 12 June 1827, 'Melancholy Death of Captain Richard Monk', and *The Oriental Herald and Journal of General Literature*, Volume 15 (ed. James Silk Buckingham).

4   Reference among family papers.

5   *Chester Courant*, 12 May 1829

6   *Chester Courant*, 15 September 1829

7   JM.07.07. Letter from Joseph Monk to sister Esther (Nessie) Matthews. 1826

8   JM.03.04. Letter from Emma de Blois Russell. 11 Sep (circa 1837)

9   JM.03.04. Letter from Emma de Blois Russell. 11 Sep (circa 1837)

10 *Chester Chronicle*, 2 Oct 1829

11 Noted down from an information stand in Neston's church of St Mary & St Helen

12 JM.02.01. Letter to Richard Grosvenor. 1820

13 JM.03.02. Letter from sister Elizabeth and Edward Acton Gibbon. 26 Nov 1827

14 JM.02.04. Edward Brace's testimony of Monk's service (copy). 5 Jun 1827

15 *Naval Biographical Dictionary*, William O'Byrne. John Murray, 1849.

16 Details from shipbuilder Kelsick Wood's journal. Privately owned.

17 Based on Kelsick Wood's shipyard ledger

18 *Gore's Liverpool General Advertiser*, 3 June 1830

19 *Isle of Man Times*, 'Presentation to the Peel lifeboat men', 9 November 1889 and *Isle of Man Examiner,* Saturday 24 October 1885

20 TNA: ADM 51/3483

21 JM.03.04. Letter from Emma de Blois Russell. 11 Sep (circa 1837)

22 *Gore's Liverpool General Advertiser*, 21 September 1837

23 JM.03.03. Letter from John Wilson Patten of Bank Hall (undated, likely 1830s)

24 *Chester Chronicle*, 26 October 1838

25 *Wexford Independent*, 8 November 1837

26 *Wexford Independent*, 8 November 1837

8. The comforts of home

1   *Chester Courant and Advertiser for North Wales*, 'A Neston Elopement', 10 July 1907
2   JM.02.08. Letter to Geo Louthean (1848)
3   JM.02.09 Letter to Geo Louthean in 1848
4   *Liverpool Mail*, 15 July 1843, p4
5   *Chester Chronicle*, 29 November 1844
6   JM.05.04. Letter from Robert Grosvenor. 11 Apr 1833
7   JM.05.06. Grosvenor to Monk (1840)
8   JM.05.07. Letter from Robert Grosvenor. 11 Jun 1840
9   JM.05.08. Letter from Grosvenor. 8 Aug 1840, and JM.05.09. Letter from Grosvenor. 16 Sep 1840
10 E. Grosvenor, *Narrative of a Yacht Voyage in the Mediterranean: During 1840-41*. Murray, 1842
11 JM.05.11. Letter from Richard Grosvenor's office
12 JM.03.02. Letter from sister Elizabeth and Edward Acton Gibbon. 26 Nov 1827
13 JM.03.05. Letter to William Brown. 19 Apr 1837
14 Ian Mitchell, *Tradition and Innovation in English Retailing*, 1700 to 1850, (Routledge, 2016), p183
15 The shop lost some of its lustre after its Victorian and Edwardian heyday, but the glass-domed roofs, chandeliers and elaborate plaster-work remained, and Browns of Chester stood as a prominent part of the city centre into the twenty-first century.
16 Joseph Hemingway, *History of the City of Chester, from Its Foundation to the Present Time*, 1831, p346
17 *Chester Chronicle*, 21 November 1845
18 JM.04.01. Letter from Nessie Brown to William Brown, 23 May 1881
19 JM.02.07. Letter to George Louthean. 27 Feb 1848
20 JM.02.07. Letter to Geo Louthean (1848)
21 JM.02.08. Letter to George Louthean (probable). 3 July 1848
22 Based on OMSA.org, 'Origins of the Military General Service Medal (1793-1814)', 2016
23 *Chester Chronicle*, 31 December 1859
24 *Liverpool Daily Post*, 8 February 1861
25 Based on *Liverpool Mercury*, 6 November 1875 and *Cheshire Observer*, 13 November 1875

26 *Wrexham Guardian*, 18 September 1875
27 *Naval & Military Gazette and Weekly Chronicle of the United Service*, 12 May 1880
28 *Cheshire Observer*, 16 May 1877
29 *Liverpool Echo*, 03 May 1880, p4
30 *Crewe Chronicle*, Saturday 08 May 1880, p6
31 *Nantwich Guardian*, 08 May 1880, p4
32 *Liverpool Echo*, 03 May 1880, p4
33 Will from General Records Office. Probate 21 May 1880. Folio 274
34 Information from NestonPast.com website. Last accessed August 2020. 'Charity of Nessie Mathews and John Monk (Mathews Monk Charity)'
35 Will from General Records Office. Probate 21 May 1880. Folio 274
36 Leach. *The Lifeboat Service in England: The North West and Isle of Man*. Amberley, 2017 and *The Graphic*, 24 October 1885

Epilogue. The Irish Sea, October 7th, 1889

1 *Isle of Man Times*, Wednesday 09 October 1889
2 Hall Caine, *The Little Manx Nation*. William Heinemann, 1891

Appendix. Untellable tales

1 *Chester Chronicle,* May 8, 1880